Quick and Easy
CROSS STITCH DESIGNS
INSPIRED BY YOUR GARDEN

Quick and Easy
CROSS STITCH DESIGNS
INSPIRED BY YOUR GARDEN

Anne and Michael Lane

THE READER'S DIGEST ASSOCIATION, INC.
Pleasantville, New York/Montreal

A Reader's Digest Book
Edited and produced by Michael O'Mara Books Limited

Photography by Helen Pask
Book Design by Clive Dorman & Co.

First published in Great Britain in 1995
The designs in this book are copyrighted and must not be stitched for resale.

Library of Congress Cataloging in Publication Data

Lane, Anne.
    Quick and easy cross stitch designs inspired by your garden / Anne
and Michael Lane.
        p.   cm.
    "First published in Great Britain in 1995"—T.p. verso
    ISBN 0-89577-857-2
    1. Cross-stitch—Patterns.   2. Gardens in Art.   I. Lane, Michael.
II. Title.
TT778.C76L373   1996
746.44'3041—dc20   95-43417

Printed in Germany

ontents

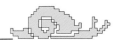

The Basics of Cross Stitch

THE FABRIC

To work cross stitch embroidery, you need to use a material that has a regular and definite weave so that you can stitch your crosses easily. You will find that there are several types which are widely available, and we have used four for the projects in this book.

1. Aida cloth

This fabric is the one most commonly used for working cross stitch, and you should be able to obtain it from any needlecraft supplier. It is a regularly woven fabric that looks like small squares with a hole at each corner, and your crosses are stitched by simply working from hole to hole diagonally across the square. Aida is available in many colors and is an extremely versatile material.

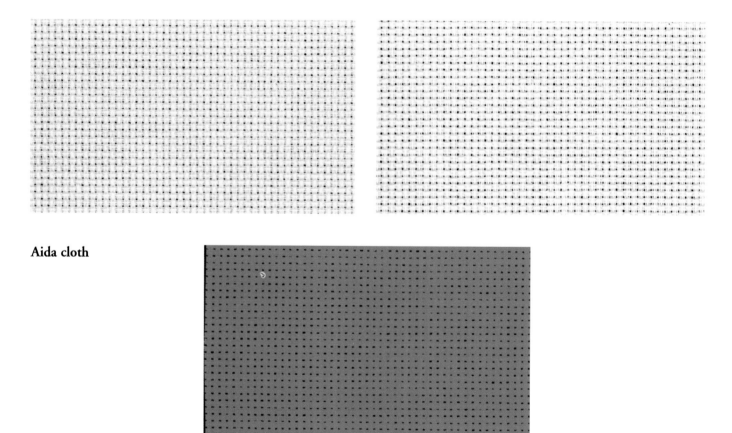

Aida cloth

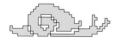

Many beginners' projects will use Aida cloth, since it is probably the easiest fabric on which to learn. It is referred to by the number of squares (and, therefore, stitches) to the inch and, of course, the more squares there are, the finer the weave will be, with the fabric becoming slightly more difficult to work. The most commonly available fabrics are 14-count Aida, which is used in many projects and kits, and 18-count Aida, which is used to achieve more detail in delicate designs.

There are several other sizes of Aida, from 5-count upward, but you may find that many Aida-type fabrics will be referred to by specific trade names.

2. Evenweave fabrics

These fabrics are very different from Aida because they are not solid weaves, but consist of threads of material regularly spaced across the length and breadth of the fabric; crosses are usually made by working diagonally across two threads (see also The Stitches, below). Some evenweave materials are available in different colors, but you will usually be required to work on white or natural colors. Antique-colored dyes have become quite popular in reproducing historical pieces.

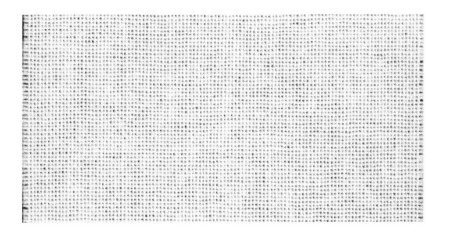

Evenweave fabrics

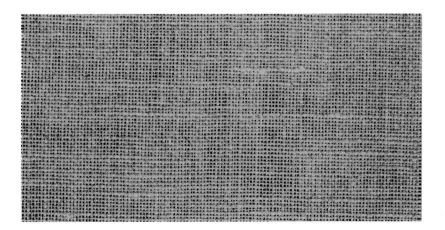

Evenweave, in both cotton and linen, can be obtained from a good supplier, but the range available may be limited. The most common weave is about 26 threads to the inch (approximately equivalent to 14-count Aida), though for finer work you will find that 28 or 32 threads to the inch is used. This type of fabric, especially evenweave linen, is more traditional than Aida and will be used in older embroidery and samplers.

Evenweave fabrics are a little more difficult to work initially, but do not be discouraged, because once you are familiar with them you will find them just as easy to stitch as cotton Aida cloth.

3. Perforated paper

This is a stiffened craft paper that has holes punched in it through which your stitches are worked. Perforated paper corresponds very closely to 14-count Aida in size, and is worked in exactly the same way, although you will need to use more strands of floss in your needle to cover the paper completely. It is very useful for stitching articles that should not lose their shape when handled, and we have used it, for example, to make a bookmark and some Christmas decorations. Perforated paper can be found at many needlework retailers or craft stores.

4. Fine canvas

Canvas is, of course, usually associated with tapestry or needlepoint work, but fine canvas (we use 18 holes to the inch) is very good for stitching projects that require a more sturdy finish, such as the change purse and the glasses case to be found in the book. It should be readily available from any needlecraft supplier.

Canvas is worked in a slightly different way from the other three materials we have used (see The Stitches, below) and, as in tapestry work, the background will always be filled in with a solid color so that no unworked canvas can be seen in the finished article. Projects using canvas can, therefore, take a little longer to complete.

PREPARING YOUR FABRIC TO START

To make sure that your embroidery is correctly positioned when you are stitching it, you must make sure that it is in the right place on your fabric. It is therefore extremely important to know where to work the first stitch, and because one of the golden rules of cross stitch embroidery is that you begin as close as you can to the center of the design, you need a simple method of determining where the center of the design should be.

Unless your project states otherwise, the center of the design will be at the center of the fabric, and if this is so, just follow these steps to find your starting point:

1. Fold your fabric in half along one side, and pinch gently to mark the central thread.
2. Baste some brightly colored cotton thread across the fabric following the line of this thread. This thread is referred to as a "guideline."
3. Repeat this process along the second side of the fabric.
4. The point where your guidelines cross will mark the center of the fabric and the point where your center stitch should be positioned.

Where a project calls for you to position the center of the design away from the center of the fabric, there will be specific instructions to follow and you will need to baste guidelines along the threads indicated by the instructions rather than along central threads.

Perforated paper

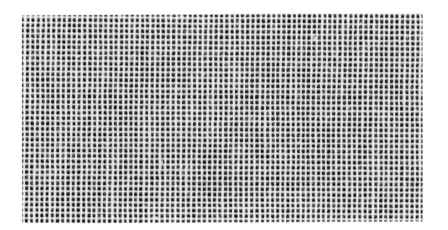

Fine canvas

After stitching your guidelines, always press the fabric carefully before you start the project and — especially if you are using an evenweave material — it is advisable to hem around the edges so that they do not fray.

Hint
Never remove your basting until the project is finished because you can use the guidelines as helpful reference points when you are working.

USING AN EMBROIDERY HOOP OR TAPESTRY FRAME

It is perfectly possible to stitch many projects without using either an embroidery hoop or a tapestry frame, but it will be much easier to keep your stitches even and result in a neater finished piece if one is used.

Embroidery hoops

Embroidery hoops come in many sizes, but you should make sure that the design fits completely inside the hoop without having to alter its position.

Traditional hoops are wooden and consist of two rings, one inside the other. An adjustable screw attachment on the outer ring is tightened to hold your fabric in place. You will also find plastic hoops that clip together to secure the fabric.

To fix your fabric in a wooden hoop

1. After basting the guidelines, place the fabric over the inner ring so that the center of the design is in the center of the ring. With the tension screw loosened, press the outer ring over it.
2. Smooth the fabric and straighten the weave before tightening the screw.
3. Fix your fabric securely enough to keep it taut, but do not stretch it too much since it is easy to distort the weave.

Hint:
To stop your fabric being marked by the friction of the hoop, lay tissue paper over it before fixing it in the outer ring. When you have tightened the screw, you can tear the paper away from the area to be embroidered.

Tapestry frames

Tapestry frames should be used if the design is too big to fit inside a hoop. There are many different types available, including hand-held and floor-standing variations. If in doubt, talk to your supplier about your requirements. Frames usually come with two rollers, with tapes attached, and two flat pieces, which hold the rollers a set distance apart.

Using a tapestry frame

1. After marking the guidelines, fix your fabric to the tapes on both rollers with basting stitches and then overcast the tapes and fabric together, keeping the fabric flat but undistorted.
2. Hem the sides of your fabric to stop them fraying on the rollers.
3. Fit the side pieces and gather up any extra fabric on to the rollers until the fabric is taut and you can easily see the area you wish to work.
4. Never leave worked fabric wound tightly to a frame for long periods, as the stitching will become flattened and lifeless.
5. If your piece of material is too small to fit the frame, you can make it larger by basting scraps of the same type of fabric to the top and bottom of your material and then fixing these to the frame.

THE COLORS

Six-strand embroidery floss is the thread most commonly used in cross stitch embroidery. It is bought in skeins about 8.7 yards (8 m) long, and there are several ranges readily obtainable. Throughout this book we have referred to the DMC range of colors, but a Conversion Table to other ranges will be found on page 123.

When you buy the floss, you will see that it is made up of six strands. You will almost always have to separate out these strands to use a smaller number when you are stitching. Most embroidery is worked with only two strands of floss in the needle, but a particular project may call for several strands, especially for backstitching. Stitching on canvas and perforated paper is always worked with three strands.

It is very important that you know how many strands you should be using. A common error beginners make is to use the wrong number of strands when stitching.

Separating the strands

Cut off a length of between 18 in (46 cm) and 24 in (61 cm) from the skein and fold it loosely in half in your hand. Gently take hold of the number of strands you need and, starting at the center, tease them completely away from the others and thread them through your needle. (Remember to use up the remaining strands from this length before cutting any more from the skein.)

Hint

Store your unused working lengths of floss on an organizer card, which you can also use for easy reference while you are stitching.

Take a piece of thin white poster board about 4 x 2 in (10 x 5 cm) and make holes down each side about ½ in (1.2 cm) apart to thread your floss through. Label each color with its number and you will not have to worry about matching the cut lengths to their skeins.

THE NEEDLE

You must use blunt-nosed tapestry needles for cross stitch embroidery. Size 24 is suitable for most projects, but you will need the smaller size 26 on finer fabrics and for detailed work, such as outlining.

Hint

If the thread becomes very twisted when you are stitching, allow the needle to dangle freely from the underside of the fabric to untwist it naturally.

THE STITCHES

The greatest attraction of cross stitch embroidery for many people is that although only a very few stitches have to be learned, so many different effects can be achieved with them. Very basic and simple projects use the same stitches as the most complex and detailed of cross stitch embroidery, and once you have mastered the stitches explained below, you will be able to work almost every cross stitch design.

Cross stitch

This stitch is, of course, the basis of all cross stitch embroidery. It is a very simple stitch to work, but to ensure that your finished piece is as attractive as possible, you should make a special effort to keep the tension of your stitches even – never pull too tight!

Making a single cross in Aida cloth or evenweave

1. Bring your needle through at A and go back into the fabric at B. As you can see, this will be a diagonal across one square on Aida cloth, or a diagonal across two threads of evenweave.
2. Move to C and bring your needle up again, then complete the cross by going back into fabric at D.

You will need to work in single stitches if the design requires you to do one of the following:
    a) stitch a color in a vertical line.
    b) stitch a color diagonally.
    c) work individual stitches at random in order to provide detail.

Make sure that after completing each stitch you begin the next one in the right place to complete your cross in the same way.

Working a row of cross stitches on Aida cloth or evenweave

When you have large areas of color to fill, you may find it easier to stitch in horizontal rows. The method below produces neat vertical lines on the reverse of the embroidery, making it easier to stretch when you have finished.

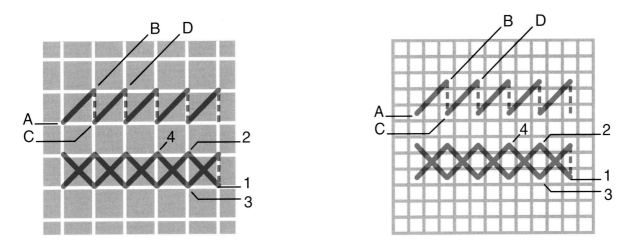

1. Work the first half of your crosses as shown (A to B, C to D, etc.) until you have counted off the number of stitches in the row.
2. Make the crosses by returning along the row in reverse (1 to 2, 3 to 4, etc.).

When you have completed one row, move to a starting position that will allow you to work the next row in the same way.

Note: The method of forming a cross which we have shown here is the one we use, but you may prefer to work your stitch in reverse, so that the top of the cross is stitched in the opposite direction. Whichever method you choose, always make sure that the top of *every* stitch in the design is stitched in the *same* direction.

Hint

When you are stitching, do not start or end your threads by knotting them behind the fabric, since this produces a very uneven surface on the finished piece.

To start stitching, hold about an inch of color in place at the back and work your first few stitches over it to anchor it in position. Then, when you have come to the end of your section or your length, weave an inch or so of floss into the back of existing stitches.

Cross stitches on perforated paper are worked in the same way as cross stitches on Aida cloth, but with three strands of floss.

Working cross stitches on canvas

The crosses are formed on canvas as they are on the other types of material, but instead of working over two threads, you work over only one intersection of canvas, using three strands of floss. This ensures that the canvas is completely covered.

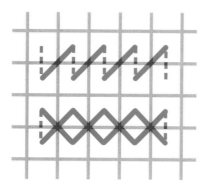

Backstitch

Almost all projects will require you to provide extra definition to parts of the design by using simple backstitch. This process is commonly known as outlining.

Never start to do any backstitching until you have completed *all* the cross stitches in a given design.

The outlining will normally be shown by a continuous line on the chart (see Design Chart, below) and you should follow this line exactly. It will often go over the top of cross stitches, and you must be certain of the number of strands you should have in your needle, since this may vary, not only from one project to another but also within the same project. The color you need for each part of the outlining will be indicated in the instructions accompanying a design.

Working backstitch

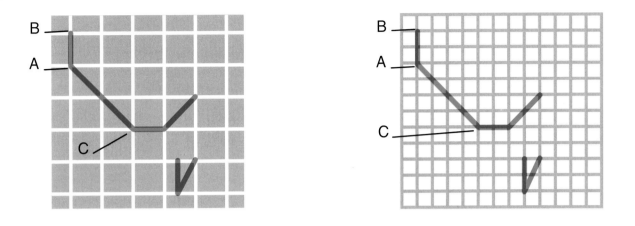

1. Start by anchoring your thread in the back of some cross stitches and then bring your needle through the fabric at a convenient point along the line (A).
2. Go back through the fabric at the beginning of the line (B).
3. Take your needle forward behind the material to another point on the line (C).
4. Bring your needle through at C and take it back again through A.
5. Continue in this way until you reach the end of the line. Then anchor your floss into the backs of cross stitches.

> **Hint**
> It is often more effective to work in longer backstitches when you are outlining over the top of cross stitches, but never make them too long or they will become very loose.

Half cross stitches and three-quarter cross stitches
As their names indicate, these stitches are based on a cross stitch but are not worked as full crosses.

A half cross stitch is complete when the first half of the standard cross has been stitched. It is shown on a chart as a diagonal line, and your stitch should be worked in the same direction as the diagonal line.
A three-quarter cross stitch is completed by working the first half of a cross, then attaching a short diagonal from the center into an opposite corner. The stitch is used to achieve a diagonal effect in a particular area of a design and is quite common. However, there are no three-quarter cross stitches in this book.

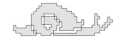

THE DESIGN CHART

In cross stitch embroidery there is no transfer pattern on the fabric for you to follow. You must stitch your design by referring to a chart, which will act as your blueprint. The important point to remember is that your stitching should correspond exactly to the design drawn on the chart.

Full-color charts are used in this book, but you will also find many black-and-white charts in use. All charts are drawn on graph paper, with the position of every cross stitch on a color chart being shown by a colored square representing the color you must use. In a black-and-white chart, the color is shown by a symbol. A Color Key accompanies each chart, explaining the use of colors and symbols.

An empty square on the chart means that no stitch is to be worked in that square.

When following color charts, an important point to realize is that the chart is not intended to be a painting of the design; it is a clear plan of the design, devised to be as easy to follow as possible. You will therefore often find that where cotton thread colors are very close, a symbol has been added to some of the colored squares to avoid confusion, and that the colors shown on the chart do not match the threads exactly.

Outside the design on the chart, there are arrows or some similar indication showing the central threads of the design. If you join these points in pencil across the chart itself, you will be able to pinpoint the center of the design exactly, and so position your first stitch on the fabric by reference to your guidelines.

> *Hint*
> To use your organizer card as effectively as possible, you can make a note beside each color of any symbol that is used to represent it on the chart. This will save you from continually searching through the Color Key.

The shape of any backstitching in a design is shown by a continuous line on the chart. If more than one color is used for outlining in a project, the details will be found in accompanying instructions and each color used for backstitching will be drawn in with a different color line. In order to show clearly on charts, the color of backstitching is often very different from the actual color used, so do not be surprised if black cotton thread is represented by a red line for example.

On black-and-white charts, it is more difficult to work out the positioning of backstitching, but different colors are often represented by different types of lines.

> *Hint*
> Some people are discouraged from taking up cross stitch because they feel that charts look difficult to follow, and that it is easy to lose track of their position. You can avoid this problem quite simply if you use a pin to show where you are.
> On a large design you may also wish to block in the areas of stitching that you have completed.

STITCHING THE DESIGN

The key to successful cross stitch embroidery lies in careful preparation and a complete understanding of the charts and techniques. When you are stitching, there are only a few very simple rules to remember, and if you follow them closely, your embroidery will be successful and attractive:

1. Start stitching at or near the center of the design and make sure that your first stitch is in the correct position on the fabric.
2. Work outward from the center so that you have to do as little counting as possible. When you have finished one section, move on to an adjoining section.
3. If you have to move across unstitched fabric, count off the stitches accurately. Take particular care when you are using an evenweave material.
4. Work the largest areas of color first, and fill in the detail later. Your embroidery will take shape more quickly, and it will be much easier to see exactly where your single stitches should go.
5. Keep the tension of your stitches as even as you can. Pull them firmly to avoid looping, but take care not to pull so tightly that you distort the weave of the fabric.
6. Complete all cross stitches (and any others in the design) before any outlining.
7. Do not trail lengths of floss behind fabric that will remain unworked, as they may well show through the piece when it is finished.
8. Enjoy yourself.

Hint

Although it is possible to hand-wash embroideries when they have been worked, it is not advisable to do so. It is far better to keep your work clean by always placing it in a cloth bag or something similar when you are not stitching.

Stop the surface of finished embroideries becoming dirty by spraying them with a suitable fabric protector.

WHEN YOU HAVE FINISHED

Cross stitch embroidery is put to many uses, and in this book we have designed projects which will enable you to learn the most common methods of finishing off smaller pieces of work so that they are displayed to the best advantage. If you ever need, for example, to place your embroidery in a card or turn it into a bookmark, you will find an example of how to do it in the following pages.

A word of warning, though. After you have stitched a large sampler or worked a beautiful fire screen, do please go to a specialist framer who is experienced in mounting embroidery to seek advice. The craft of stretching large pieces of work properly is a skilled one and takes much practice.

Kingfisher Picture

Very rarely, when it is very quiet, this sleek and elegant bird can be glimpsed at rest, sunning himself on a branch overhanging the river. Work this colorful design and then mount it for all to see in the hoop that you have used to stitch it.

YOU WILL NEED

to make one design size 3½ x 3¼ in (9 x 8.2 cm) approx.

To stitch the design

5 in (12.7 cm) traditional wooden embroidery hoop
10 x 10 in (25.4 x 25.4 cm) white Aida cloth (14-count)
1 x 8.7 yd (8 m) skein of DMC 6-strand embroidery
   floss in each of the 14 colors listed in the Color Key
Size 24 tapestry needle
Colored cotton thread for marking the guidelines

To display the finished piece

10 x 10 in (25.4 x 25.4 cm) white felt
White cotton thread
Sharp sewing needle
Scissors
Fabric glue (optional)

STITCHING THE DESIGN

1. Baste guidelines with colored cotton thread to mark the center of the Aida cloth before positioning it on hoop.
2. Join the arrows on the chart to find the center of the design and stitch the piece, using two strands of floss for all cross stitches. Outlining details are included.
3. Remove the Aida from the hoop (do not take out the guidelines!) and steam-press the worked piece flat after placing it facedown on a clean surface. If you are not using a steam iron, lay a damp cloth over the wrong side of the Aida before pressing it.

DISPLAYING THE PIECE

1. Use the outside of the hoop's inner ring as a template to cut out a circle of white felt for the backing.
2. Position the design centrally in the hoop, using the guidelines to help you place it correctly.
3. Take out the guidelines.
4. Trim away excess Aida from behind the hoop, leaving about 1 in (2.5 cm) all around.
5. Work a row of running stitches in white cotton thread about ½ in (1.2 cm) from the cut edge of the fabric and gather them tightly before tying off the thread. The edges of the Aida should now be lying within the thickness of your hoop.
6. Place the white felt circle over the back of the hoop, making sure it lies as flat as possible on the inner ring.
7. Fix the felt to the Aida, using either a suitable glue or a few stitches worked around the edge.

COLOR KEY						
⊟		Blanc	8	943	Bright Jade
☐	310	Black	6	991	Dark Jade
9	317	Dark Gray	1	992	Jade Green
2	318	Gray	Ⅲ	993	Pale Jade
⸬	351	Coral Pink	7	3022	Dark Stone
⊟	436	Golden Tan	5	3024	Stone
3	738	Pale Tan	⊠		1 strand of 991 with 1 strand of 992
4	798	Cobalt Blue			

OUTLINING

▬▬▬ Use one strand of 310 Black around the eye.

▬▬▬ Use one strand of 317 Dark Gray at the neck.

Country Pot Holder

You'll be amazed how easy it is to make this useful pot holder decorated with marjoram from the herb garden.

YOU WILL NEED

to make one pot holder, finished size 6 x 6 in (15.2 x 15.2 cm) approx.

To stitch the design

8 x 8 in (20.3 x 20.3 cm) white Aida cloth (14-count)
1 x 8.7 yd (8 m) skein of DMC 6-strand embroidery floss in each of the 6 colors listed in the Color Key
Size 24 tapestry needle
Colored cotton thread for marking the guidelines

To make the pot holder

7 x 7 in (18 x 18 cm) quilted backing fabric of your choice
1 yd (0.9 m) green bias binding, ⅝ in (1.4 cm) wide
Green cotton thread to match your binding
Sharp sewing needle
Pins
Scissors

STITCHING THE DESIGN

1. Baste guidelines with colored cotton thread to mark the center of the Aida before positioning it on your hoop or frame. This design will fit into a 6 in (15.2 cm) embroidery hoop.
2. Join the arrows on the chart to find the center of the design and stitch the piece, using two strands of floss for all cross stitches. No backstitching is required.
3. Remove the guidelines and steam press the worked piece flat after placing it facedown on a clean surface. If you are not using a steam iron, lay a damp cloth over the wrong side of the Aida before pressing it.

MAKING THE POT HOLDER

1. Turn the design faceup, and trim the Aida to 7 x 7 in (18 x 18 cm), making sure that the design remains centrally positioned.
2. Turn the design facedown and lay the quilted fabric on top of it.
3. Join the fabrics together with basting stitches all around, taking a ½ in (1.2 cm) seam from every side. Hand or machine-stitch along the seam and then remove the basting.
4. Trim the seam allowance to ¼ in (6 mm) wide.
5. Attach the bias binding to the pot-holder (*see 8 below*), starting at the top left-hand corner of the Aida and continuing around all sides. When you have returned to your starting-point, measure another 2¼ in (5.7 cm) of binding before cutting off the excess.
6. Slip-stitch the long edges of binding together, and form a loop, folding the raw end under ¼ in (6 mm).
7. Fix the loop to the quilted side of the pot holder, using small stitches for the best result.
8. **To attach bias binding**
a) Open out the folded edge on one edge of the binding, and pin it in position on the right side of the fabric, matching the edge of the binding to the raw edges of the seam allowance(s). Secure the binding by hand or machine-stitching along the seamline(s).
b) Fold the binding over the raw edges onto the wrong side of the fabric, and hold it in position with pins or basting stitches before neatly hemming it to finish.

COLOR KEY						
⊟	597	Turquoise	1	704	Bright Leaf Green	
Ⅱ	598	Pale Turquoise	3	962	Carmine Rose Pink	
2	701	Dark Bright Green	4	3350	Old Carmine Rose	

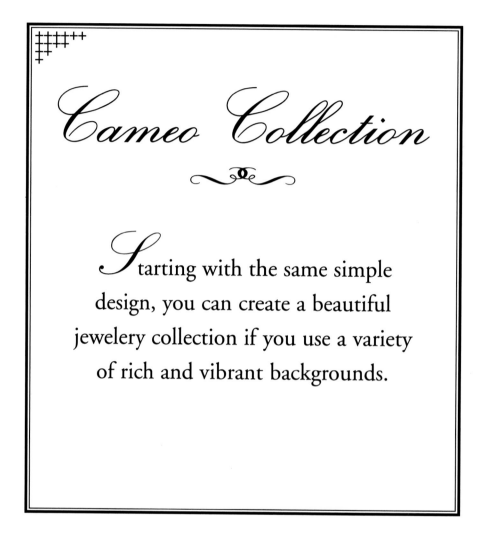

Cameo Collection

Starting with the same simple design, you can create a beautiful jewelery collection if you use a variety of rich and vibrant backgrounds.

YOU WILL NEED

to make one brooch or pendant, finished size 1⅝ x 1½ in (4 x 3.8 cm) approx.

(The chart shows three variations of the design with different backgrounds. Each design will fit any of the brooch mounts.)

To stitch the design once

5 x 5 in (12.7 x 12.7 cm) white single thread interlock canvas (18 holes to the inch)

1 x 8.7 yd (8 m) skein of DMC 6-strand embroidery floss in 5 of the colors listed in the Color Key

Size 26 tapestry needle

Colored cotton thread for marking the guidelines

To assemble a brooch or pendant

3 x 3 in (7.6 x 7.6 cm) medium-weight iron-on white interfacing

White poster board

Pins

Scissors

Black background as shown: 1⅝ x 1³⁄₁₆ in (4 x 3 cm) purchased antique gold frame

Mauve background as shown: 1⅝ x 1¼ in (4 x 3.1 cm) purchased gold metal brooch

Old Rose Pink pendant: 1⅝ x 1¼ in gold frame purchased 24 in (61 cm) gilt chain

STITCHING THE DESIGN ONCE

1. Baste guidelines with colored cotton thread to mark the center of the canvas. You should find that the canvas is stiff enough to work in your hand, but you may wish to fix it to a small tapestry frame. Do not use an embroidery hoop!
2. Join the arrows on the chart to find the center of the design and stitch the piece, using three strands of floss for all cross stitches. No backstitching is required.
3. Stitch each cross stitch over one intersection of canvas only (see The Basics of Cross Stitch, page 14).
4. Remove the guidelines and gently ease the worked piece flat and square by pulling at each corner. You should not use steam on canvas unless it has been properly blocked by a professional stretcher.

ASSEMBLING A BROOCH OR PENDANT

1. With the design facedown, iron the interfacing onto the wrong side of the canvas, making sure that you cover all the stitching. The interfacing adds stability to the canvas and also prevents stitches from fraying when you trim the design to fit the brooch mount.
2. Use the acetate provided with the mount to draw a template that can be used to trim the design to the correct size. Place the acetate on white poster board and draw around it in pencil.
3. Cut out the template around the inside edge of the pencil line and pin it securely on top of your design so that the same amount of stitching shows on all sides.
4. Trim around the template as carefully as you can.
5. Finish assembling the brooch or pendant by following the supplier's instructions.

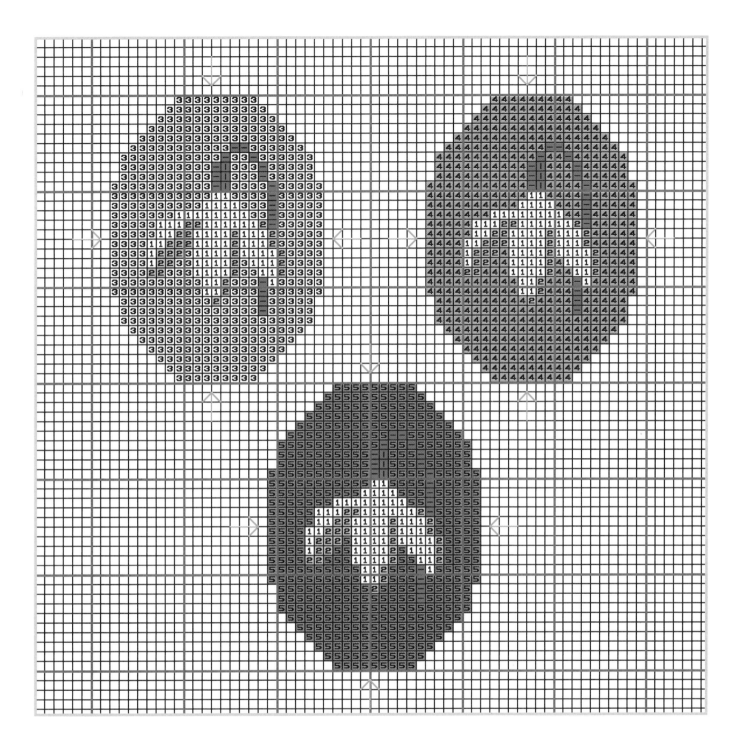

COLOR KEY					
①		Blanc	▧	700	Dark Emerald Green
③	310	Black	▬	702	Emerald Green
⑤	327	Mauve	④	956	Old Rose Pink
②	415	Pale Gray			

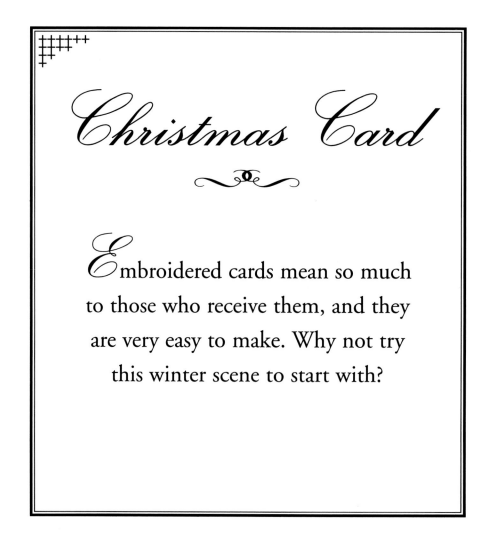

Christmas Card

Embroidered cards mean so much to those who receive them, and they are very easy to make. Why not try this winter scene to start with?

YOU WILL NEED

to make one card, with a design size 2½ x 2 in (6.3 x 5 cm) approx.

To stitch the design

6 x 6 in (15.2 x 15.2 cm) white Aida cloth (18-count)
1 x 8.7 yd (8 m) skein of DMC 6-strand embroidery floss in each of the 13 colors listed in the Color Key
Size 26 tapestry needle
Colored cotton thread for marking the guidelines

To assemble the card

6 x 6 in (15.2 x 15.2 cm) medium-weight iron-on white interfacing
Double-faced tape, ½ in (1.2 cm) wide
Trifold card with opening 3½ x 3 in (9 x 7.6 cm) approx.
Scissors

STITCHING THE DESIGN

1. Baste guidelines with colored cotton to mark the center of the Aida before positioning it on your hoop or frame. This design will fit into a 5 in (12.7 cm) embroidery hoop.
2. Join the arrows on the chart to find the center of the design and stitch the piece, using two strands of floss for all cross stitches. Outlining details are included.
3. Remove the guidelines and steam-press the worked piece flat after placing it facedown on a clean surface. If you are not using a steam iron, lay a damp cloth over the wrong side of the Aida before pressing it.

ASSEMBLING THE CARD

1. After pressing your worked piece, leave it facedown and iron the interfacing onto it.
2. Place the opening of the card over the design, and trim the stiffened Aida. Keep the design centrally positioned and cut the fabric so that it overlaps the opening by at least ¾ in (2 cm) on each side.
3. Put strips of double-faced tape around the inside of the card, near to each edge of the opening, and then position the taped side of the card over the design and press it down on to the fabric. Do not press too firmly until your design is in the right place.
4. Lay the design facedown, with the holly nearest to you, and fix strips of double-faced tape on the left-hand leaf of the card. Press this tape firmly down onto the central leaf to hide the Aida.

COLOR KEY						
7		Blanc	6	642	Dark Stone
1	310	Black	9	702	Emerald Green
3	318	Gray	III	703	Bright Leaf Green
4	420	Wood Brown	2	712	Pale Linen
5	422	Cinnamon	=	947	Orange Coral
8	434	Dark Wood Brown	II	3341	Coral
=	608	Orange Flame			

OUTLINING

Use one strand of 310 Black for the beak and around the eye.

Use one strand of 318 Gray around the snow on top of the post.

Summertime
Picture

❦

*I*n the still, hazy heat of midsummer, a tortoiseshell butterfly flutters gently toward a clump of wild flowers, preparing to alight undisturbed.

YOU WILL NEED

to make one design size 3½ x 3½ in (9 x 9 cm) approx.

To stitch the design

10 x 10 in (25.4 x 25.4 cm) white Aida cloth (14-count)
1 x 8.7 yd (8 m) skein of DMC 6-strand embroidery
    floss in each of the 15 colors listed in the Color Key
    and Outlining
Size 24 tapestry needle
Colored cotton thread for marking the guidelines

To mount the embroidery

5½ x 5½ in (14 x 14 cm) white mounting board
Pins
Double-faced tape, ½ in (1.2 cm) wide
Masking tape, 1 in (2.5 cm) wide

STITCHING THE DESIGN

1. Baste guidelines with colored cotton thread to mark
   the center of the Aida before positioning it on your
   hoop or frame. This design requires an embroidery
   hoop of at least 6 in (15.2 cm).
2. Join the arrows on the chart to find the center of the
   design and stitch the piece, using two strands of floss
   for all cross stitches. Outlining details are included.
3. Do not remove the guidelines, but steam-press the
   worked piece flat after placing it facedown on a clean
   surface. If you are not using a steam iron, lay a damp
   cloth over the wrong side of the Aida before pressing.

MOUNTING THE EMBROIDERY

1. Trim the Aida to 7½ x 7½ in (19 x 19 cm), making
   sure that the design remains centrally positioned.
2. With the design facedown, center the mounting
   board over the Aida. To do this, mark the midpoint
   on all four sides of the board and align these points
   with the guidelines on your fabric.
3. Place a pin into the thickness of the board at each of
   these four points, joining the Aida and the board
   together. Turn the board over so that you can see the
   embroidery.
4. Starting at the top of the design, insert pins at regular
   intervals into the thickness of the board to stretch the
   Aida. Work from the midpoint out to each side, and
   keep the fabric as flat and square as you can. This is
   done by keeping the thread of Aida nearest to the
   edge as straight as possible, and pulling the fabric so
   that it lies flat but does not distort.
5. Repeat the process around the other three sides of the
   design (working top-side-bottom-side), but on these
   sides work from a pinned corner to the opposite
   corner. You may find that your central pins will need
   to be moved as the embroidery is stretched.
6. When you have pinned all four sides, make any necessary adjustments, remove the guidelines, and place the
   design facedown.
7. Cut a strip of double-faced tape 5½ in (14 cm) long,
   and lay it along the top edge of the board. Fold the
   Aida over so that it is held securely by the tape.
   Repeat the process around the other three sides (working top-bottom-side-side). The corners will have an
   extra thickness, but keep them as flat as you can.
8. Cover the raw edges of the fabric with strips of masking tape and remove all pins.

This method of mounting embroidery is suitable for
small designs, such as those in this book. If you wish to
mount large designs, or embroidery worked on heavy-
weight fabrics, we recommend that the work be done by
a professional stretcher and framer, who will probably
use lacing thread.

OUTLINING

Use one strand of 209 Dark Lilac around the flowers.
Use one strand of 987 Dark Leaf Green for the leaf veins.
Use one strand of 3031 Peat Brown for the butterfly's antennae.
Use one strand of 420 Wood Brown around the edges of the wings.

COLOR KEY					
4		Blanc	6	740	Bright Orange
‖	210	Lilac	7	741	Orange
≡	211	Pale Lilac	8	989	Leaf Green
−	420	Wood Brown	5	996	Bright Turquoise
I	433	Dark Brown	2	3031	Peat Brown
3	445	Deep Lemon	9	3348	Moss Green
1	738	Pale Tan			

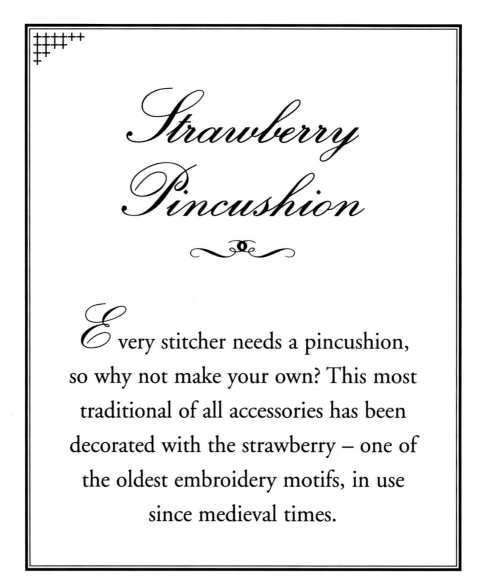

Strawberry Pincushion

*E*very stitcher needs a pincushion, so why not make your own? This most traditional of all accessories has been decorated with the strawberry – one of the oldest embroidery motifs, in use since medieval times.

YOU WILL NEED

to make one pincushion, finished size 3¾ x 3¾ in (9.5 x 9.5 cm) approx.

To stitch the design

6 x 6 in (15.2 x 15.2 cm) white single-thread interlock canvas (18 holes to the inch)

1 x 8.7 yd (8 m) skein of DMC 6-strand embroidery floss in each of the colors listed in the Color Key, except shade 798 Cobalt Blue

4 x 8.7 yd (8 m) skeins of DMC 6-strand embroidery floss, shade 798 Cobalt Blue

Size 24 tapestry needle

Colored cotton thread for marking the guidelines

To make the pincushion

6 x 6 in (15.2 x 15.2 cm) blue velvet fabric

Batting or polyester stuffing

Blue cotton thread to match your velvet

Sharp sewing needle

Pins

Scissors

STITCHING THE DESIGN

1. Baste guidelines with colored cotton thread to mark the center of the canvas. You should find that the canvas is stiff enough to work it in your hand, but you may wish to fix it to a small tapestry frame. Do not use an embroidery hoop!

2. Join the arrows on the chart to find the center of the design and stitch the piece, using three strands of floss for all cross stitches. No backstitching is required.

3. Stitch each cross stitch over one intersection of canvas only (see The Basics of Cross Stitch, page14).

4. Remove the guidelines and gently ease the worked piece flat and square by pulling at each corner. You should not use steam on canvas unless it has been properly blocked by a professional stretcher.

MAKING THE PINCUSHION

1. Measure ½ in (1.2 cm) away from the stitching on all four sides and trim the canvas to size. Cut blue velvet to same size by laying it on top of canvas.

2. Place the two fabrics right sides together and join them with basting stitches all around, taking a ½ in (1.2 cm) seam from every side. Leave an opening of about 2 in (5 cm) along one side so that you can pad out the pincushion with batting. Hand-or machine-stitch along the seam, then remove the basting.

3. Trim the seam allowance close to the seam itself and turn the pincushion right side out, making sure that the seams lie as flat as possible inside.

4. Insert batting or stuffing to the required firmness and finish by slipstitching your opening closed along the stitching line.

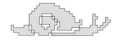

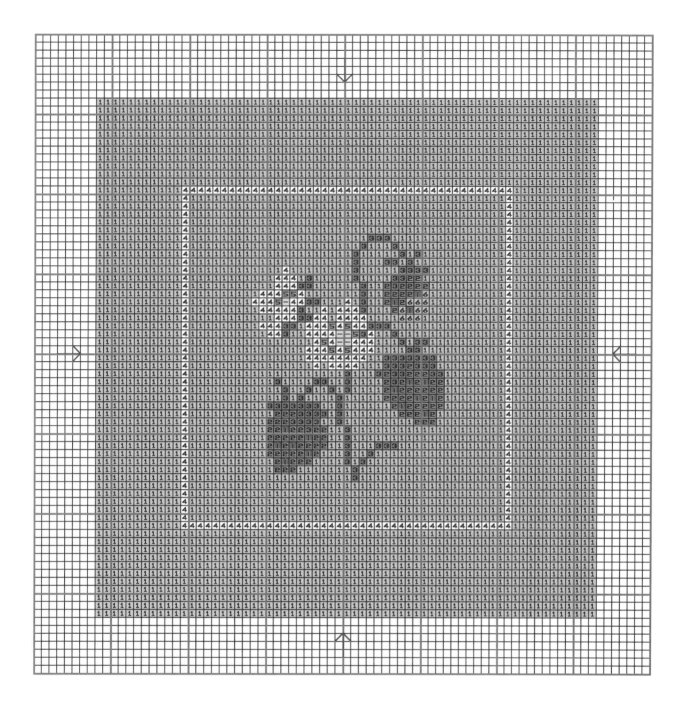

COLOR KEY					
4		Blanc	3	703	Brilliant Green
1	351	Coral	5	740	Orange
6	352	Strawberry Pink	1	798	Cobalt Blue
2	606	Flame Red	−	973	Bright Yellow

Country Cottage Sampler

The most popular form of decorative embroidery is the sampler – this colorful and modern version is inspired by a pretty little English cottage.

YOU WILL NEED

to make one design size 6½ x 5½ in (16.5 x 14 cm) approx.

To stitch the design

12 x 11 in (30.5 x 28 cm) cream Aida cloth (14-count)
1 x 8.7 yd (8 m) skein of DMC 6-strand embroidery
    floss in each of the 11 colors listed in the Color Key
Size 24 tapestry needle
Colored cotton for marking the guidelines

To mount the embroidery

8½ x 7½ in (21.5 x 19 cm) white mounting board
Pins
Double-faced tape, 1 in (2.5 cm) wide
Masking tape, 1 in (2.5 cm) wide

STITCHING THE DESIGN

1. Baste guidelines with colored cotton thread to mark the center of the Aida before positioning it on your frame. This design does not fit comfortably into an embroidery hoop.
2. Join the arrows on the chart to find the center of the design and stitch the piece, using two strands of floss for all cross stitches. Outlining details are included.
3. Do not remove the guidelines, but steam press the worked piece flat after placing it facedown on a clean surface. If you are not using a steam iron, lay a damp cloth over the wrong side of the Aida before pressing.

MOUNTING THE EMBROIDERY

1. Trim the Aida to 10½ x 9½ in (26.7 x 24 cm), making sure that the design remains centrally positioned.
2. With the design facedown, place the mounting board centrally over the Aida. To do this, mark the midpoint on all four sides of the board, and align these points with the guidelines on your fabric.
3. Place a pin into the thickness of the board at each of these four points, joining the Aida and the board together. Turn the board over so that you can see the embroidery.
4. Starting at the top of the design, place pins at regular intervals into the thickness of the board to stretch the Aida. Work from the midpoint to each side, and keep the fabric as flat and square as you can. This is done by keeping the thread of Aida nearest to the edge as straight as possible, and pulling the fabric so that it lies flat but does not distort.
5. Repeat the process around the other three sides of the design (*working top-side-bottom-side*), but on these sides work from a pinned corner to the opposite corner. You may find that your central pins will need to be moved as the embroidery is stretched.
6. When you have pinned all four sides, make any necessary adjustments, remove the guidelines, and place the design facedown.
7. Cut a strip of double-faced tape 8½ in (21.5 cm) long, and lay it along the top edge of the board. Fold the Aida over so that it is held securely by the tape. Then repeat the process around the other three edges (*working top-bottom-side-side*), with the tape at the two sides being 7½ in (19 cm) long. The corners will have an extra thickness, but try to keep them flat.
8. Cover the raw edges of the fabric with strips of masking tape and remove all pins.

This method of mounting embroidery is suitable for small designs, such as those in this book. If you wish to mount large designs, or embroidery worked on heavy-weight fabrics, we recommend that the work be done by a professional stretcher and framer, who will probably use lacing thread.

COLOR KEY					
6		Blanc	7	644	Dark Linen
−	210	Lilac	9	676	Golden Straw
3	310	Black	8	680	Dark Gold
4	351	Deep Coral	5	890	Dark Forest Green
I	367	Forest Green	2	3064	Brick
1	420	Wood Brown			

OUTLINING

Use one strand of 310 Black for all outlining on the cottage.

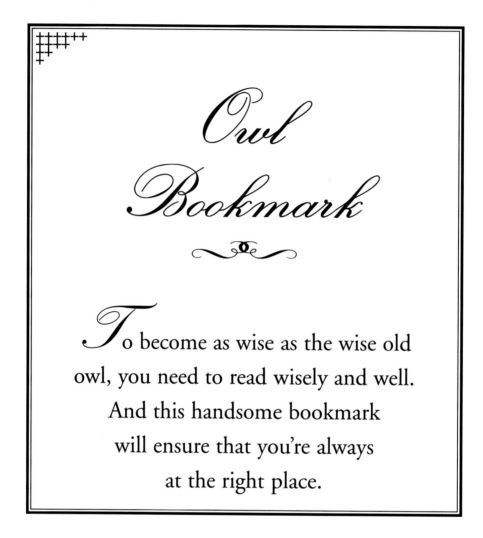

Owl Bookmark

To become as wise as the wise old
owl, you need to read wisely and well.
And this handsome bookmark
will ensure that you're always
at the right place.

YOU WILL NEED

to make one bookmark, finished size 5½ x 2¾ in (14 x 7 cm) approx., plus ribbon

To stitch the design

7½ x 4½ in (19 x 11.5 cm) white perforated paper (14 holes to the inch).
1 x 8.7 yd (8 m) skein of DMC 6-strand embroidery floss in each of the 13 colors listed in the Color Key
Size 24 tapestry needle
Colored cotton thread for marking the guidelines

To make the bookmark

6 x 3 in (15.2 x 7.6 cm) medium-weight iron-on white interfacing
12 in (30.5 cm) double-faced green satin ribbon, ½ in (1.2 cm) wide
Pins
Scissors

STITCHING THE DESIGN

1. Baste guidelines with colored cotton thread to mark the center of the paper. You will need to do this by counting, as the paper must not be folded.
2. Work the design in your hand; do not use a hoop or embroidery frame.
3. Join the arrows on the chart to find the center of the design and stitch the piece, using three strands of floss for all cross stitches. Outlining details are included.
4. Perforated paper does not require pressing. Remove the guidelines.

MAKING THE BOOKMARK

1. Mark the cutting line on to the right side of the design, and carefully trim the bookmark to size.
2. Turn the design facedown and trim the interfacing so that there will be a border of one stitch of paper showing at each edge when the interfacing is ironed into place. Put the interfacing to one side.
3. Press the ribbon in half, and with the design face-down, pin it into position near the bottom right-hand corner of the perforated paper, so that ½ in (1.2 cm) of the ribbon will lie beneath the interfacing.
4. Iron the interfacing onto the wrong side of the paper, positioning it carefully. Make sure that the ribbon is securely fixed. Then remove the pin.
5. Trim each end of the ribbon streamer by cutting a small V shape into each end.

COLOR KEY					
▥	301	Pale Chestnut Brown	⑦	612	Stone
⑥	310	Black	⑤	644	Dark Linen
⑨	400	Chestnut Brown	②	741	Bright Orange
①	436	Golden Tan	④	822	Linen
⊟	535	Dark Gray	⊟	3021	Dark Chocolate
⑧	610	Chocolate Brown	⑧	3033	Pale Stone
▯	611	Stone Brown			

OUTLINING

━━ Use three strands of 610 Chocolate Brown for all outlining.
━━ The red line on the chart indicates the cutting line.

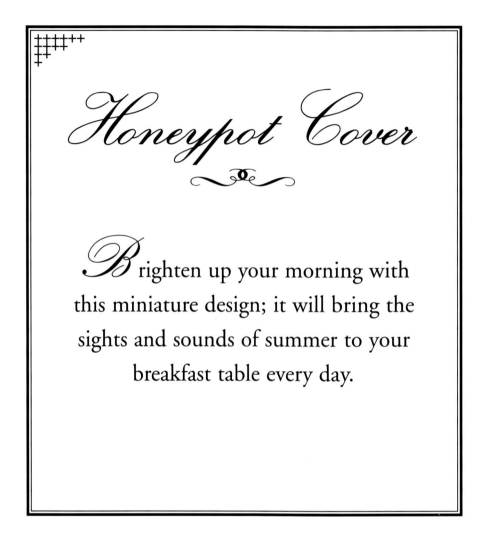

Honeypot Cover

Brighten up your morning with this miniature design; it will bring the sights and sounds of summer to your breakfast table every day.

YOU WILL NEED

to make one cover, finished size 6 x 6 in (15.2 x 15.2 cm) approx.

To stitch the design

8 x 8 in (20.3 x 20.3 cm) white Aida cloth (18-count)
1 x 8.7 yd (8 m) skein of DMC 6-strand embroidery
    floss in each of the 10 colors listed in the Color Key
    and Outlining
Size 26 tapestry needle
Colored cotton thread for marking the guidelines

To make the cover

White cotton thread
Sharp sewing needle
Pins
Scissors
Glass jar with lid
Thin white rubber band
24 in (61 cm) narrow double-faced green satin ribbon

STITCHING THE DESIGN

1. Baste guidelines with colored cotton thread to mark
   the center of the Aida before positioning it on your
   hoop or frame. This design will fit into a 5 in (12.7
   cm) embroidery hoop.
2. Join the arrows on the chart to find the center of the
   design and stitch the piece, using two strands of floss
   for all cross stitches. Outlining details are included.
3. Remove the guidelines and steam press the worked
   piece flat after placing it facedown on a clean surface.
   If you are not using a steam iron, lay a damp cloth
   over the wrong side of the Aida before pressing it.

MAKING THE COVER

1. Measure 1 in (2.5 cm) from the edge of the Aida
   around all four sides, and baste new guidelines along
   the nearest threads.
2. Place pins at the four points where these guidelines
   cross, then remove the basting.
3. Starting at a pin, work a square in blanketstitch with
   the pins at each corner.
4. Remove the pins and trim around the outside of the
   blanketstitch, cutting one Aida square away from the
   stitching.
5. Center the design over the lid of the glass jar and hold
   the fabric in place with the rubber band. Ease the
   Aida gently so that it lies flat on the lid.
6. Tie the ribbon around the jar, making sure that it
   covers the rubber band completely.

COLOR KEY						
☑		Blanc	☑	701	Bright Green	
①	310	Black	⬛	792	Deep Blue	
⑤	351	Deep Coral	④	813	China Blue	
Ⅲ	434	Dark Wood Brown	⑦	966	Pale Laurel	
−	437	Harvest Gold				

OUTLINING

— Use one strand of 434 Dark Wood Brown around the hive.

— Use one strand of 699 Dark Bright Green for the flower stems.

Christmas Tree Decorations

As Christmas draws near, gather the holly and the ivy from the countryside, and find a tree to bring home. We hope these three colorful hanging decorations will add a sparkle to your celebrations.

YOU WILL NEED

to make three decorations, finished size 3 x 3 in (7.6 x 7.6 cm) approx., plus ribbon

To stitch the design

3 pieces of white perforated paper (14 holes to the inch) cut to 4½ x 4½ in (11.5 x 11.5 cm)

1 x 8.7 yd (8 m) skein of DMC 6-strand embroidery floss in the two colors listed in the Color Key

Mez Diadem Gold Metallic floss (shade 0300) or similar

Size 24 tapestry needle

Colored cotton thread for marking the guidelines

To make the decorations

3 pieces medium-weight iron-on white interfacing cut to 3 x 3 in (7.6 x 7.6 cm)

3 yds (2.7 m) gold ribbon, ⅛ in or 3 mm wide

White cotton thread

Sharp sewing needle

Pins

Scissors

Double-faced tape, ½ in (1.2 cm) wide

STITCHING THE DESIGNS

1. Baste guidelines with colored cotton thread to mark the center of a piece of paper. You will need to do this by counting, as the paper must not be folded.
2. Work the design in your hand; do not use a hoop or frame.
3. Join the arrows on the chart to find the center of the design and stitch the piece, using three strands of floss for all cross stitches. Outlining details are included.
4. The metallic floss is worked in straight stitch or half cross stitch as shown on the charts. Make sure that it lies as flat as possible.
5. Perforated paper does not require pressing. Leave the guidelines in position.

MAKING EACH DECORATION

1. Mark the cutting line on the right side of the design and carefully trim the decoration to size.
2. Turn the design facedown and trim the interfacing so that it slightly overlaps your stitching when it is ironed into place. Put the interfacing to one side.
3. Take 1 yd of ribbon and cut two lengths of 15 in (38 cm) from it. Fold one piece of ribbon in half to form a loop, and catch the ends together with a stitch. Turn the design facedown and center the loop at the top of the design so that its end will lie ½ in (1.2 cm) beneath the interfacing. Hold it in position with a pin and remove the guidelines.
4. Iron the interfacing onto the back of the design, positioning it carefully. Make sure that the ribbon is securely fixed, then remove the pin.
5. Make a bow from the second length of ribbon and trim the ends to your chosen length.
6. Turn the design faceup, and center a small piece of double-faced tape at the top (where the loop meets the paper). Press the bow firmly onto the tape.

COLOR KEY					
▆	606	Bright Red	Ⅱ	701	Bright Green

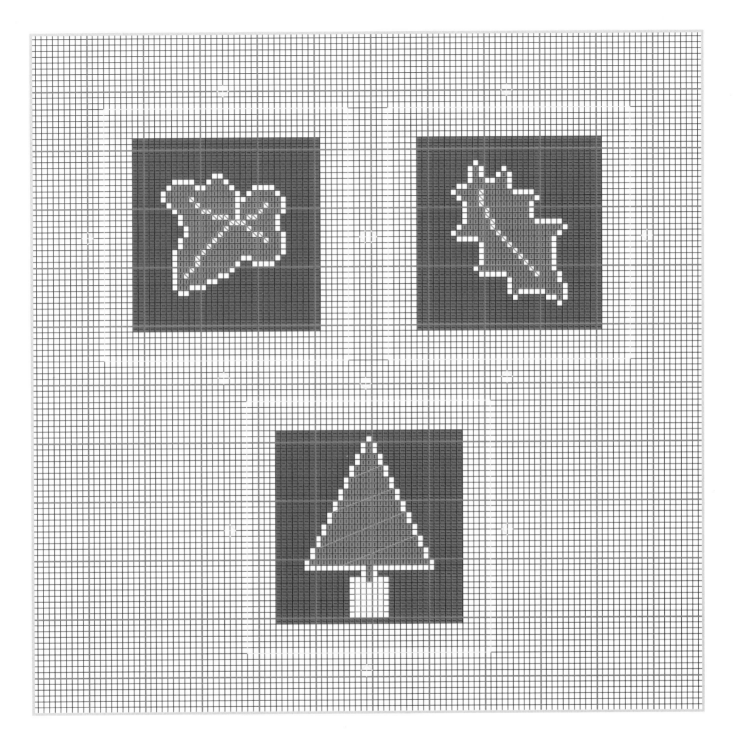

OUTLINING

On the two leaves, work the Gold Metallic floss as half cross stitches sloping in the direction indicated.

On the tree, work the Gold Metallic floss streamers as single straight stitches.

The tree tub is worked by stitching six horizontal straight stitches.

The yellow line on each chart indicates the cutting line.

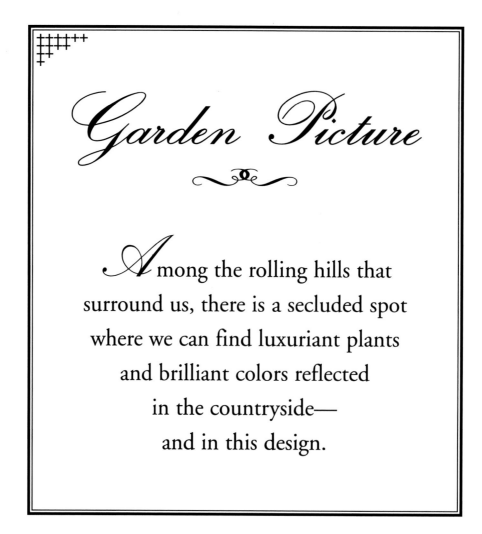

Garden Picture

Among the rolling hills that
surround us, there is a secluded spot
where we can find luxuriant plants
and brilliant colors reflected
in the countryside—
and in this design.

YOU WILL NEED

to make one design size 4½ x 2¼ in (11.5 x 5.7 cm) approx.

To stitch the design

10 x 8 in (25.4 x 20.3 cm) white Aida cloth (14-count)
1 x 8.7 yd (8 m) skein of DMC 6-strand embroidery
    floss in each of the 12 colors listed in the Color Key
Size 24 tapestry needle
Colored cotton thread for marking the guidelines

To mount the embroidery

6½ x 4¼ in (16.5 x 10.7 cm) white mounting board
Pins
Double-faced tape, ½ in (1.2 cm)wide
Masking tape, 1 in (2.5 cm) wide

STITCHING THE DESIGN

1. Baste guidelines with colored cotton thread to mark the center of the Aida before positioning it on your hoop or frame. This design requires at least a 6 in (15.2 cm) embroidery hoop.
2. Join the arrows on the chart to find the center of the design and stitch the piece, using two strands of floss for all cross stitches.
3. Do not remove the guidelines, but steam press the worked piece flat after placing it facedown on a clean surface. If you are not using a steam iron, lay a damp cloth over the wrong side of the Aida before pressing it.

MOUNTING THE EMBROIDERY

1. Trim the Aida to 8½ x 6¼ in (21.5 x 15.9 cm), making sure that the design is centered.
2. With the design facedown, place the mounting board centrally over the Aida. To do this, mark the midpoint on all four sides of the board, and align these points with the guidelines on your fabric.
3. Place a pin into the thickness of the board at each of these four points, joining the Aida and the board together. Turn the board over so that you can see the embroidery.
4. Starting at the top of the design, place pins at regular intervals into the thickness of the board to stretch the Aida. Work from the midpoint out to each side, and keep the fabric as flat and square as you can. This is done by keeping the thread of Aida nearest to the edge as straight as possible, and pulling the fabric so that it lies flat but does not distort.
5. Repeat the process around the other three sides of the design (working top-side-bottom-side), but on these sides work from a pinned corner to the opposite corner. You may find that your central pins will need to be moved as the embroidery is stretched.
6. When you have pinned all four sides, make any necessary adjustments, remove the guidelines, and place the design facedown.
7. Cut a strip of double-faced tape 6½ in (16.5 cm) long, and lay it on the board along one of the sides. Fold the Aida over so that it is held securely by the tape. Repeat the process around the other three sides (working side-side-top-bottom), with the tape at the top and bottom being 4¼ in (10.7 cm) long. The corners will have an extra thickness, but try to keep them as flat as you can.
8. Cover the raw edges of the fabric with strips of masking tape and remove all pins. The design will be shown to best effect in a picture mount that slightly overlaps the stitches around all four sides.

This method of mounting embroidery is suitable for small designs, such as those in this book. If you wish to mount large designs, or embroidery worked on heavy-weight fabrics, we recommend that the work be done by a professional stretcher and framer, who will probably use lacing thread.

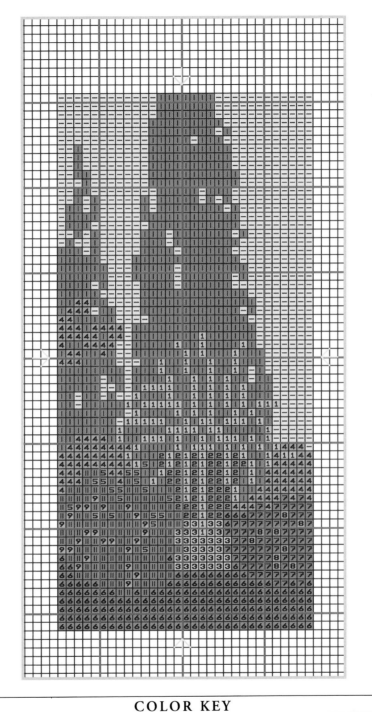

COLOR KEY					
▥	367	Forest Green	▤	922	Terra-cotta
①	369	Pale Forest Green	⑤	956	Old Rose
▥	470	Bright Green	⑥	989	Grass Green
⊟	747	Sky Blue	⑦	3345	Dark Green
⑨	772	Wood Green	④	3348	Moss Green
③	842	Stone	⑧	3609	Cyclamen

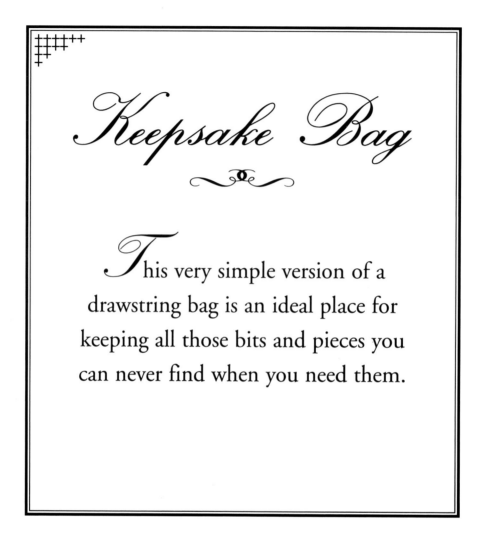

Keepsake Bag

*T*his very simple version of a drawstring bag is an ideal place for keeping all those bits and pieces you can never find when you need them.

YOU WILL NEED

to make one bag, finished size 6 x 4 in (15.2 x 10 cm) approx.

To stitch the design

9 x 7¼ in (22.9 x 18.3 cm) white evenweave cotton (26 threads to the inch)

1 x 8.7 yd (8 m) skein of DMC 6-strand embroidery floss in each of the 9 colors listed in the Color Key

Size 24 tapestry needle

Colored cotton thread for marking the guidelines

To make the bag

White cotton thread

Sharp sewing needle

30 in (76 cm) thin white cording

Pins

Scissors

STITCHING THE DESIGN

1. Place the evenweave so that its long side runs from left to right. Mark the vertical guideline of the design by measuring in 2½ in (6.3 cm) from the right-hand edge and following the thread nearest to this point.

2. To mark the second guideline, measure up 2¾ in (7 cm) from the bottom of the fabric and follow the nearest thread. The design is stitched in the right-hand half of the fabric only, with the point where your guidelines cross being the point where the center of the design is positioned.

3. If you fix this design to a hoop, take special care not to mark the fabric. It may be better to use a small tapestry frame.

4. Join the arrows on the chart to find the center of the design and stitch the piece, using two strands of floss for all cross stitches. Outlining details are included.

5. Remove the guidelines and steam-press the worked piece flat after placing it facedown on a clean surface. If you are not using a steam iron, lay a damp cloth over the wrong side of the fabric before pressing it.

MAKING THE BAG

1. Measure down ¾ in (2 cm) from the top of the fabric and, following the nearest thread, mark a new guideline from left to right. Mark another guideline 1¼ in (3.1 cm) from the top. These guidelines indicate the casing for your cording.

2. With the design faceup, fold the evenweave in half so that the right sides are together; the stitched design is covered by the left-hand side of the fabric. All the work on this project is done on the wrong side.

3. Taking a ½ in (1.2 cm) seam, join the side and bottom together with basting stitches, but leave the space between your two guidelines open. Hand- or machine-stitch along the seam and remove the basting stitches. Trim the seam allowance to ¼ in (6 mm).

4. Fold a small hem along a thread about ¼ in (6 mm) from the top of your bag and press it flat.

5. Form the casing by folding over the new upper edge along your top guideline. Pin it in place, and remove both guidelines.

6. Stitch around the casing, working as close as you can to the pressed edge, then turn the bag right side out. Make sure that all seams lie as flat as possible.

7. Insert the cording into the casing, pulling the ends to an even length, and knot the ends together.

<table>
<tr><td colspan="6" align="center">COLOR KEY</td></tr>
<tr><td>⊟</td><td>435</td><td>Golden Brown</td><td>☑</td><td>891</td><td>Deep Pink</td></tr>
<tr><td>Ⅱ</td><td>472</td><td>Pale Spring Green</td><td>❸</td><td>956</td><td>Old Rose</td></tr>
<tr><td>❻</td><td>552</td><td>Dark Violet</td><td>❹</td><td>957</td><td>Fuchsia Pink</td></tr>
<tr><td>❺</td><td>553</td><td>Violet</td><td>❶</td><td>989</td><td>Leaf Green</td></tr>
</table>

OUTLINING

══ Use one strand of 956 Old Rose for the flower stamens.

━━ Use one strand of 987 Dark Leaf Green for the leaf veins.

Valentine Gift

$\mathcal{A}$ heart to stitch is
a token of love, a treasure to
be kept forever.

YOU WILL NEED

to make one heart, finished size 4½ x 4½ in (11.5 x 11.5 cm) approx.

To stitch the design

8 x 8 in (20.3 x 20.3 cm) white evenweave cotton (26 threads to the inch)

1 x 8.7 yd (8 m) skein of DMC 6-strand embroidery floss in each of the 3 colors listed in the Color Key

DMC Fil Or Clair [Gold Metallic floss]

Size 24 tapestry needle

Colored cotton thread for marking the guidelines

To make the heart

2 pieces of plain white cotton fabric (e.g., cotton lawn), both 8 x 8 in (20.3 x 20.3 cm)

7 in (18 cm) gold ribbon, ¼ in (6 mm) wide

Batting or polyester stuffing

White cotton thread

Sharp sewing needle

Pins

Pinking shears

STITCHING THE DESIGN

1. Baste guidelines with colored cotton thread to mark the center of the evenweave before positioning it on your hoop or frame. This design will fit into a 6 in (15.2 cm) embroidery hoop.
2. Join the arrows on the chart to find the center of the design and stitch the piece, using two strands of floss for all cross stitches. Outlining details are included.
3. Remove the guidelines and steam-press the worked piece flat after placing it facedown on a clean surface. If you are not using a steam iron, lay a damp cloth over the wrong side of the evenweave before pressing it.

MAKING THE HEART

1. With the design lying faceup on top, pin all three pieces of fabric together, 2 in (5 cm) from each edge.
2. Fold the ribbon in half to form a loop, and catch the ends together with a stitch. Place the loop between the two pieces of plain white fabric so that its end lies behind the gold heart on the design. Hold it in position with a pin.
3. Baste through all three layers, ⅛ in (3 mm) away from the edge of the design, making sure that you catch the ribbon in place. Leave an opening of about 2 in (5 cm) along one side so that you can pad out the heart with batting or stuffing.
4. Working just outside the basting stitches, hand- or machine-stitch around the design, then remove basting. (Remember to leave an opening!).
5. Trim around the heart with pinking shears, ⅜ in (9 mm) from your stitching line. Be careful not to cut through the ribbon – you will need to pink both in front and behind it.
6. Pad the heart with batting between the two pieces of plain fabric, and finish by slipstitching your opening closed along the stitching line.

COLOR KEY					
⊟	368	Pale Forest Green	☒	680	Dark Gold
1	519	Turquoise Blue	⊡		Gold Metallic floss

OUTLINING

Use two strands of 680 Dark Gold for the beaks.

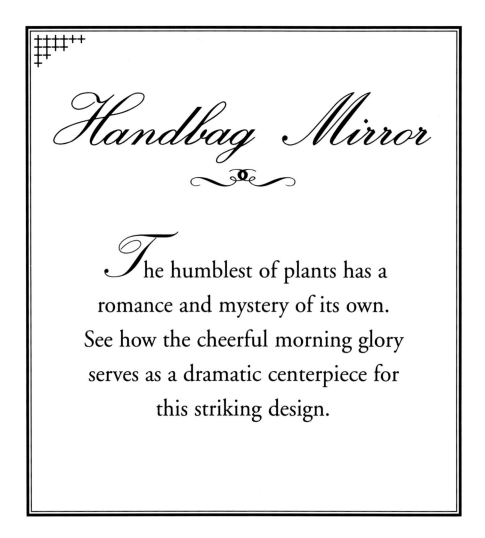

Handbag Mirror

The humblest of plants has a
romance and mystery of its own.
See how the cheerful morning glory
serves as a dramatic centerpiece for
this striking design.

YOU WILL NEED
to make one mirror, 2⅝ in (6.7 cm) round

To stitch the design
7 x 7 in (18 x 18 cm) white Aida cloth (18-count)
1 x 8.7 yd (8 m) skein of DMC 6-strand embroidery
  floss in each of the 5 colors listed in the Color Key
Size 26 tapestry needle
Colored cotton thread for marking the guidelines

To assemble the mirror
4 x 4 in (10 x 10 cm) medium-weight iron-on black
  interfacing
White poster board
Pins
Scissors
2⅝ in diameter (6.5 cm) purchased round handbag mirror.

STITCHING THE DESIGN
1. Baste guidelines with colored cotton thread to mark
   the center of the Aida before positioning it on your
   hoop or frame. This design will fit into a 5 in (12.7
   cm) embroidery hoop.
2. Join the arrows on the chart to find the center of the
   design. Stitch, using two strands of floss for all cross
   stitches. There is no outlining on this design.
3. Remove the guidelines and steam-press the worked
   piece flat after placing it facedown on a clean surface.
   If you are not using a steam iron, lay a damp cloth
   over the wrong side of the Aida before pressing it.

ASSEMBLING THE MIRROR
1. With the design facedown, iron the interfacing onto
   the wrong side of the Aida, making sure that you
   cover all the stitching. The interfacing adds stability
   to the fabric and also prevents stitches from fraying
   when you trim the design to fit the mirror.
2. Make a template of your mirror by placing the rim
   faceup on white poster board and drawing around the
   inside edge of the rim. If you draw around the
   outside, the design will not fit the mirror without
   distortion.
3. Cut out the template and pin it securely on top of
   your design so that the same amount of stitching
   shows on all sides.
4. Trim around the template as carefully as you can.
5. Finish assembling the mirror by following the
   supplier's instructions.

COLOR KEY					
③		Blanc	Ⅰ	743	Yellow
⊟	310	Black	1	800	Glazed Blue
❷	703	Brilliant Green			

Potpourri Sachet

Keep one of these small bags in a drawer of your dressing table to make everything sweet-smelling. Or, with its delicate lace trimming, it would be a wonderful gift.

YOU WILL NEED

to make one sachet, finished size (including lace trim)
7½ x 4½ in (19 x 11.5 cm) approx.

To stitch the design

9 x 6½ in (22.9 x 16.5 cm) white evenweave cotton (26
    threads to the inch)
1 x 8.7 yd (8 m) skein of DMC 6-strand embroidery
    floss in each of the 12 colors listed in the Color Key
Size 24 tapestry needle
Colored cotton thread for marking the guidelines

To make the sachet

Another 9 x 6½ in (22.9 x 16.5 cm) piece of white even-
    weave cotton (26 threads to the inch)
White cotton thread
Sharp sewing needle
12 in (30.5 cm) white lace trimming, ½ in (1.2 cm) wide
About 24 in (61 cm) narrow double-faced white satin
    ribbon
Pins
Scissors
Potpourri

STITCHING THE DESIGN

1. Mark the vertical guideline by folding the short side
   of the fabric in half and following the central thread.
2. To mark the horizontal guideline, measure up 2¼ in
   (5.7 cm) from the bottom of the evenweave and
   follow the thread nearest to this point. You will see
   that the design is largely stitched in the bottom half
   of the fabric, as the point where your guidelines cross
   remains the point where the center of the design
   should be positioned.
3. If you fix this design to a hoop, take special care not
   to mark the fabric. It may be better to use a small
   tapestry frame.
4. Join the arrows on the chart to find the center of the
   design and stitch the piece, using two strands of floss
   for all cross stitches. Outlining details are included.
5. Remove the guidelines and steam press the worked
   piece flat after placing it facedown on a clean surface.
   If you are not using a steam iron, lay a damp cloth
   over the wrong side of the fabric before pressing it.

MAKING THE SACHET

1. Turn the design faceup and lay the second piece of
   fabric on top of it.
2. Join the pieces of fabric together by basting stitches
   along the sides and bottom, taking about a 1 in (2.5
   cm) seam from the edge. Hand- or machine-stitch
   along the seam and remove the basting stitches.
3. Trim the seam allowances to about ½ in (1.2 cm)
   wide, and turn the sachet right side out. Make sure
   that the seams lie as flat as possible inside the sachet.
4. Turn over 1 in (2.5 cm) of fabric into the top of the
   sachet and hold it in place by basting stitches near the
   new top edge.
5. Measure the lace trimming against the top of the
   sachet and pin the two short edges of the lace
   together to mark the exact length.
6. Make a small seam at the pin and trim off excess lace
   to within about ¼ in (6 mm) before folding the two
   ends backward and pressing the seam open.
7. Turn the seam inside and pin the trimming to the top
   of the sachet, along the inside edge. Baste stitches to
   hold it in place, then remove the pins.
8. Working from the right side of the fabric, hand- or
   machine-stitch the trimming in place, sewing close to
   the top edge. Remove all basting.
9. Partially fill the sachet with potpourri and tie the
   ribbon twice around the sachet just above the
   potpourri, finishing with a bow in front.

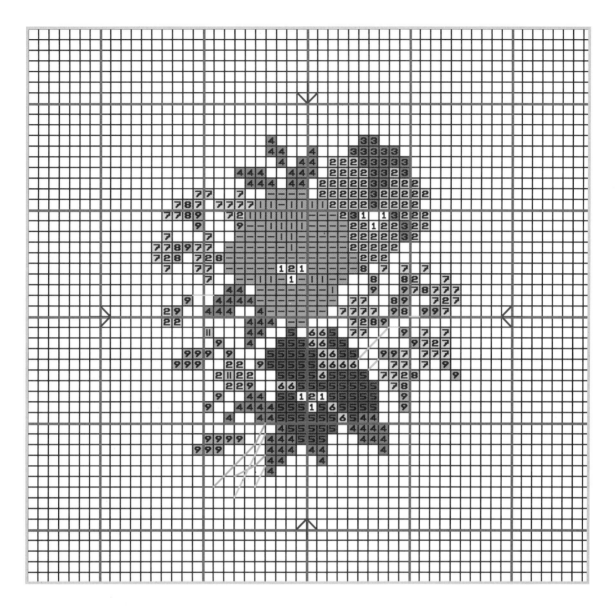

COLOR KEY						
1	310	Black		2	725	Yellow
5	333	Deep Periwinkle Blue		III	782	Burnished Gold
6	341	China Blue		3	783	Old Gold
8	604	Rose Pink		9	966	Pale Laurel
7	605	Pale Rose		4	988	Leaf Green
—	718	Raspberry		II	3608	Cyclamen Pink

OUTLINING

Use two strands of 966 Pale Laurel for the stems

Use two strands of 988 Leaf Green for the stems

Kitten
Picture

❦

Very small and very naughty,
Mitten is usually to be found hiding
under a bush, waiting for the
birds to come along.

YOU WILL NEED

to make one design size 2 x 1⅞ in (5 x 4.7 cm) approx.

To stitch the design

5 x 5 in (12.7 x 12.7 cm) white Aida cloth (14-count)
1 x 8.7 yd (8 m) skein of DMC 6-strand embroidery
    floss in each of the 10 colors listed in the Color Key
    and Outlining
Size 24 tapestry needle
Colored cotton thread for marking the guidelines

To mount the embroidery

3¼ x 3⅛ in (8.2 x 7.9 cm) white mounting board
Pins
Double-faced tape, ½ in (1.2 cm) wide
Masking tape, 1 in (2.5 cm) wide

STITCHING THE DESIGN

1. Baste guidelines with colored cotton thread to mark
   the center of the Aida before positioning it on your
   hoop or frame. This design will fit into a 4 in (10 cm)
   hoop.
2. Join the arrows on the chart to find the center of the
   design and stitch the piece, using two strands of floss
   for all cross stitches. Outlining details are included.
3. Do not remove the guidelines, but steam press the
   worked piece flat after placing it facedown on a clean
   surface. If you are not using a steam iron, lay a damp
   cloth over the wrong side of the Aida before pressing.

MOUNTING THE EMBROIDERY

1. Trim the Aida to 4¼ x 4⅛ in (10.7 x 10.5 cm),
   making sure that the design is centered.
2. With the design facedown, center the mounting
   board over the Aida. To do this, mark the midpoint
   on all four sides of the card, and align these points
   with the guidelines on your fabric.
3. Place a pin into the thickness of the board at each of
   these four points, joining the Aida and the board
   together. Turn the board over so that you can see the
   embroidery.
4. Starting at the top of the design, place pins at regular
   intervals into the thickness of the board to stretch the
   Aida. Work from the midpoint out to each side, and
   keep the fabric as flat and square as you can. This is
   done by keeping the thread of Aida nearest to the
   edge as straight as possible and pulling the fabric so
   that it lies flat but does not distort.
5. Repeat the process around the other three sides of the
   design *(working top-side-bottom-side)*, but on these
   sides work from a pinned corner to the opposite
   corner. You may find that your central pins will need
   to be moved as the embroidery is stretched.
6. When you have pinned all four sides, make any necessary adjustments, remove the guidelines, and place the
   design facedown.
7. Cut a strip of double-faced tape 3¼ in (8.2 cm) long,
   and lay it along the top edge of the board. Fold the
   Aida over so that it is held securely by the tape, then
   repeat the process around the other three edges *(working top-bottom-side-side)*, with the tape at the two
   sides being 3⅛ in (7.9 cm) long. The corners will have
   an extra thickness, but keep them as flat as you can.
8. Cover the raw edges of the fabric with strips of masking tape and remove all pins. The design will be
   shown to best effect in a small picture mount that
   slightly overlaps the stitches around all four sides.

This method of mounting embroidery is suitable for
small designs, such as those in this book. If you wish to
mount large designs, or embroidery worked on heavy-
weight fabrics, we recommend that the work be done by
a professional stretcher and framer, who will probably
use lacing thread.

COLOR KEY

2	316	Strawberry	5	778	Light Strawberry
6	318	Gray	−	993	Jade
1	613	Stone	3	3012	Dark Stone
⊡	645	Medium Gray	7	3047	Fawn
4	746	Pale Toffee			

OUTLINING

— Use two strands of 535 Dark Gray for the pupils of the eyes.

— Use one strand of 535 Dark Gray for all other outlining.

Anniversary Rose Card

The rose is a universal symbol of romance; you can send this card to remind someone of your love.

YOU WILL NEED

to make one card, with a design size 3 x 2 in (7.6 x 5 cm) approx.

To stitch the design

7 x 6 in (18 x 15.2 cm) white Aida cloth (14-count)
1 x 8.7 yd (8 m) skein of DMC 6-strand embroidery floss in each of the 6 colors listed in the Color Key
Size 24 tapestry needle
Colored cotton thread for marking the guidelines

To assemble the card

7 x 6 in (18 x 15.2 cm) medium-weight iron-on white interfacing
Double-faced tape, ½ in (1.2 cm) wide
Trifold card with opening 4 x 3 in (10 x 7.6 cm)
Scissors

STITCHING THE DESIGN

1. Baste guidelines with colored cotton thread to mark the center of the Aida before positioning it on your hoop or frame. This design will fit into a 6 in (15.2 cm) embroidery hoop.
2. Join the arrows on the chart to find the center of the design and stitch the piece, using two strands of floss for all cross stitches.
3. Remove the guidelines and steam-press the worked piece flat after placing it facedown on a clean surface. If you are not using a steam iron, lay a damp cloth over the wrong side of the Aida before pressing it.

ASSEMBLING THE CARD

1. After pressing your worked piece, leave it facedown and iron on the interfacing for stiffening.
2. Place the opening of the card over the design, and trim the stiffened Aida. Keep the design centrally positioned and cut the fabric so that it overlaps the opening by at least ¾ in (2 cm) on each side.
3. Put strips of double-faced tape around the inside of the card, near each edge of the opening, then position the taped side of the card over the design and press it onto the fabric. Do not press too firmly until you are sure that your design is in the right place.
4. Lay the work facedown, with the bottom of the design nearest you, and fix strips of double-faced tape on the left-hand leaf of the card. Press this tape firmly down on the central leaf to hide the Aida.

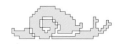

COLOR KEY

3	562	Dark Laurel Green	1	3705	Dark Coral Rose
2	563	Laurel Green	I	3706	Coral Rose
4	564	Pale Laurel Green	—	3708	Pale Coral Rose

Lavender Sachet

A complete alphabet accompanies this old favorite. Personalizing this delicate piece will transform it into a very special gift indeed.

YOU WILL NEED

to make one sachet, finished size 4½ x 3¼ in (11.5 x 8.2 cm) approx.

To stitch the design

8 x 6¾ in (20.3 x 17.1 cm) white evenweave cotton (26 threads to the inch)

1 x 8.7 yd (8 m) skein of DMC 6-strand embroidery floss in each of the 6 colors listed in the Color Key

Size 24 tapestry needle

2 lengths of different-colored cotton thread for marking guidelines

To make the sachet

5½ x 4¼ in (14 x 10.7 cm) fine white cotton fabric (e.g., cotton lawn)

36 in (91.4 cm) white lace, 1 in (2.5 cm) wide approx. *(This will be gathered.)*

White cotton thread

Sharp sewing needle

Pins

Scissors

For the padding

2 pieces of plain white cotton lawn fabric, both 5½ x 4¼ in (14 x 10.7 cm)

Batting or polyester stuffing

Lavender

STITCHING THE DESIGN

1. To be sure that the motifs are worked in the correct position, you will need to mark guidelines on your fabric showing the perimeter of your working area. To do this, measure in 1¾ in (4.5 cm) from each edge of the evenweave, and baste guidelines in colored cotton thread [Color A] along the nearest threads. You will have a rectangle of 4½ x 3¼ in (11.5 x 8.2 cm) in the center of the fabric.

2. To mark guidelines indicating the centers of the motifs, measure in 2¾ in (7 cm) from the bottom and the two sides of the evenweave, and baste guidelines in a different colored cotton thread [Color B] along the nearest threads. Measure 2⅝ in (6.7 cm) from the top and baste a fourth guideline in the same color. The points where the guidelines in Color B cross at top left and bottom right are the points where your stitching should be centered.

3. Join the arrows on the chart to find the center of the floral motif, then stitch it in the bottom right-hand corner of the fabric, using two strands of floss for all cross stitches. There is no outlining on this motif.

4. To position your initial correctly, plot it in the empty box on the chart, with the left-hand edge of the letter touching the left-hand edge of the box. The letters vary in width, and you may find that the central vertical guideline (shown by an arrow on the chart) does not pass through the center of your letter. Do not be concerned about this, but stitch the letter as you have plotted it, using two strands of floss.

5. Remove the guidelines in Color B only and steam-press the worked piece flat after placing it facedown on a clean surface. If you are not using a steam iron, lay a damp cloth over the wrong side of the evenweave before pressing it.

MAKING THE SACHET

1. Trim the evenweave to 5½ x 4¼ in (14 x 10.7 cm), keeping the working area centrally positioned.

2. Join the cut ends of the lace together with a small seam, and gather the lace until it fits neatly around the working area. Place the lace on the right side of the evenweave, with its straight edge lying just outside the guidelines. Baste the lace into position, then hold in place by hand-stitching. Remove the lace basting.

3. Place the evenweave (with lace attached) facedown on top of the backing material so that the right sides are together. Following the guidelines, pin a seamline joining the fabrics around the edge of the working area, leaving an opening of about 2 in (5 cm) along the bottom. Remove the guidelines.

4. Working just outside the pins, hand or machine-stitch the seam. Trim the seam allowance to ½ in (1.2 cm) and remove the pins.

5. Turn the fabrics right side out and insert the padding (see below) into the sachet through the opening. Slipstitch the opening closed along the seamline.

6. **To make the padding**

a) Place the two pieces of cotton lawn together and stitch a seam ½ in (1.2 cm) from every side, leaving a 2 in (5 cm) opening along one side to insert the filling. Trim the seam allowance to ¼ in (6 mm) and turn the fabric right side out.

b) Fill the pad with batting and lavender to your required thickness and slipstitch the opening closed.

COLOR KEY					
■	553	Violet	4	776	Strawberry Pink
⊟	554	Pale Violet	3	3345	Dark Green
1	727	Spring Yellow	2	3347	Green

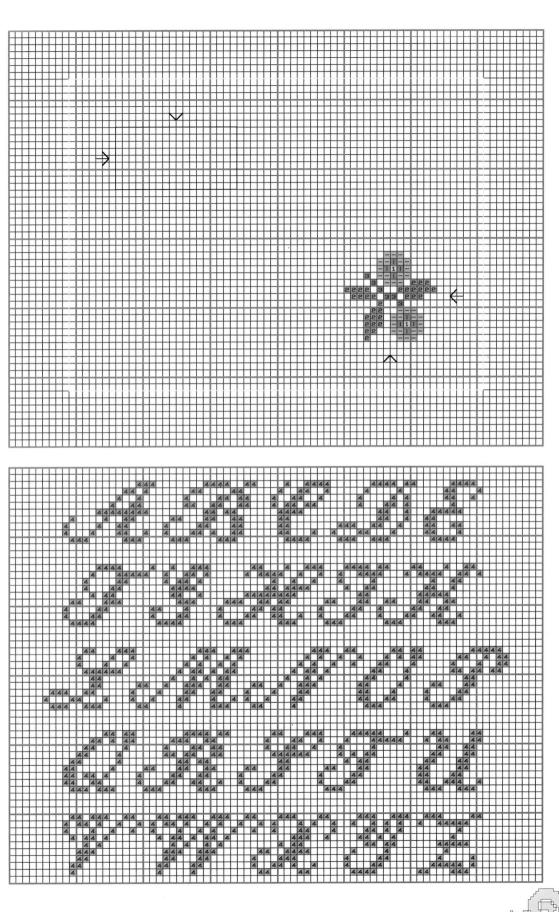

Squirrel Change Purse

Every autumn the squirrels busily gather up acorns and shrewdly stash them away for winter food. Be equally wise and store your mad money in this charming change purse.

YOU WILL NEED

to make one purse, finished size 4 x 3 in (10 x 7.6 cm) approx.

To stitch the design

2 pieces of white single thread interlock canvas (18 holes to the inch) cut to 6 x 6 in (15.2 x 15.2 cm)

1 x 8.7 yd (8 m) skein of DMC 6-strand embroidery floss in each of the colors listed in the Color Key, except shade 310 Black

6 x 8.7 yd (8 m) skeins of DMC stranded embroidery cotton, shade 310 Black

Size 24 tapestry needle

Colored cotton thread for marking the guidelines

To make the purse

2 pieces of medium-weight iron-on black interfacing cut to 6 x 6 in (15.2 x 15.2 cm)

Double-faced tape, ½ in (1.2 cm) wide

4 in (10 cm) black zipper

Black cotton thread

Sharp sewing needle

Scissors

STITCHING THE DESIGN

1. Baste one piece of canvas, and baste guidelines with colored cotton thread to mark the center. You should find that the canvas is stiff enough to work it in your hand, but you may wish to fix it to a small tapestry frame. Do not use an embroidery hoop!

2. Join arrows on chart to find center of design. Stitch the piece, using three strands of floss for all cross stitches. Outlining details are included.

3. Stitch each cross stitch over one intersection of canvas only (see The Basics of Cross Stitch, page 14)

4. To stitch the back of the purse, find the center of the second piece of canvas. Using a 310 Black, work a rectangle of cross stitches measuring 75 stitches by 56 stitches.

5. Remove the guidelines from both pieces of canvas, and gently ease them flat and square by pulling at each corner. You should not use steam on canvas unless it has been professionally blocked.

MAKING THE PURSE

1. Start with the front of the purse. Measure ½ in (1.2 cm) away from the stitching on all four sides and trim the canvas to size.

2. Turn the design facedown, and place a strip of double-faced tape along the ½ in (1.2 cm) edges for turning at both the top and bottom of the canvas. Fold the edges for turning down behind the stitching, making sure that the tape holds securely. Tape down the edges for turning at the sides in the same way.

3. Place one piece of interfacing over the canvas, trim it to size, and then iron it onto the wrong side of the canvas. (Remember not to use steam.)

4. Repeat steps 1–3 above with the back of the purse.

5. Turn the front of the purse facedown and position the zipper, also right side down, along the top edge, basting stitches ⅛ in (3 mm) from the top. Hand- or machine-stitch the zipper in place, working close to the basting stitches, then remove the basting.

6. Put the two pieces of canvas right sides together and, with the back of the purse on top, fix the zipper in place on the second piece of canvas.

7. If the ends of the zipper overlap the canvas at the sides, fold them into the inside of the purse and catch them with small stitches.

8. Turn the purse right sides out and overcast the front and back sections together. Overcast using three strands of 310 Black.

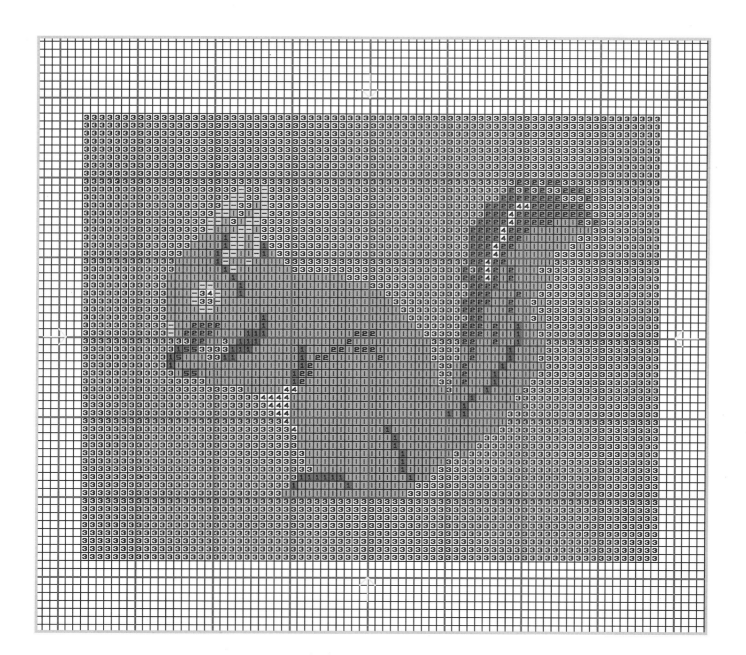

<table>
<tr><td colspan="6" align="center">COLOR KEY</td></tr>
<tr><td>4</td><td></td><td>Blanc</td><td>5</td><td>701</td><td>Bright Green</td></tr>
<tr><td>1</td><td>301</td><td>Chestnut</td><td>–</td><td>945</td><td>Bronze Flesh</td></tr>
<tr><td>3</td><td>310</td><td>Black</td><td>I</td><td>976</td><td>Russet Brown</td></tr>
<tr><td>2</td><td>402</td><td>Pale Chestnut</td><td></td><td></td><td></td></tr>
</table>

OUTLINING

—— Use one strand of 310 Black around the eye.

Poinsettia Picture

The vivid petals of this Christmas favorite make a wonderful subject for a cross stitch picture, which can be enjoyed throughout the year.

YOU WILL NEED

to make design size 2¾ x 2¾ in (7 x 7 cm) approx.

To stitch the design

9 x 9 in (22.9 x 22.9 cm) white Aida cloth (18-count)
1 x 8.7 yd (8 m) skein of DMC 6-strand embroidery
    floss in each of the 9 colors listed in the Color Key
    and Outlining
Size 26 tapestry needle
Colored cotton thread for marking the guidelines

To mount the embroidery

5 x 5 in (12.7 x 12.7 cm) white mounting board
Pins
Double-faced tape, ½ in (1.2 cm) wide
Masking tape, 1 in (2.5 cm) wide

STITCHING THE DESIGN

1. Baste guidelines with colored cotton thread to mark
   the center of the Aida before positioning it on your
   hoop or frame. This design will fit into a 6 in (15.2
   cm) embroidery hoop.
2. Join the arrows on the chart to find the center of the
   design and stitch the piece, using two strands of floss
   for all cross stitches. Outlining details are included.
3. Do not remove the guidelines, but steam-press the
   worked piece flat after placing it facedown on a clean
   surface. If you are not using a steam iron, lay a damp
   cloth over the wrong side of the Aida before pressing.

MOUNTING THE EMBROIDERY

1. Trim the Aida to 7 x 7 in (18 x 18 cm), making sure
   that the design remains centrally positioned.
2. With the design facedown, center the mounting
   board over the Aida. To do this, mark the midpoint
   on all four sides of the card, and align these points
   with the guidelines on your fabric.
3. Place a pin into the thickness of the board at each of
   these four points, joining the Aida and the board
   together. Turn the board over so that you can see the
   embroidery.
4. Starting at the top of the design, insert pins at regular
   intervals into the thickness of the board to stretch the
   Aida. Work from the midpoint out to each side, and
   keep the fabric as flat and square as you can. This is
   done by keeping the thread of Aida nearest the edge
   as straight as possible, and pulling the fabric so that it
   lies flat but does not distort.
5. Repeat the process around the other three sides of the
   design (working top-side-bottom-side), but on these
   sides work from a pinned corner to the opposite
   corner. You may find that your central pins will need
   to be moved as the embroidery is stretched.
6. When you have pinned all four sides, make any necessary adjustments, remove the guidelines, and place the
   design facedown.
7. Cut a strip of double-faced tape 5 in (12.7 cm) long,
   and lay it along the top edge of the board. Fold the
   Aida over so that it is held securely by the tape, then
   repeat the process around the other three sides (working top-bottom-side-side). The corners will have an
   extra thickness, but keep them as flat as you can.
8. Cover the raw edges of the fabric with strips of masking tape and remove all pins.

This method of mounting embroidery is suitable for
small designs, such as those in this book. If you wish to
mount large designs, or embroidery worked on heavy-
weight fabrics, we recommend that the work be done by
a professional stretcher and framer, who will probably
use lacing thread.

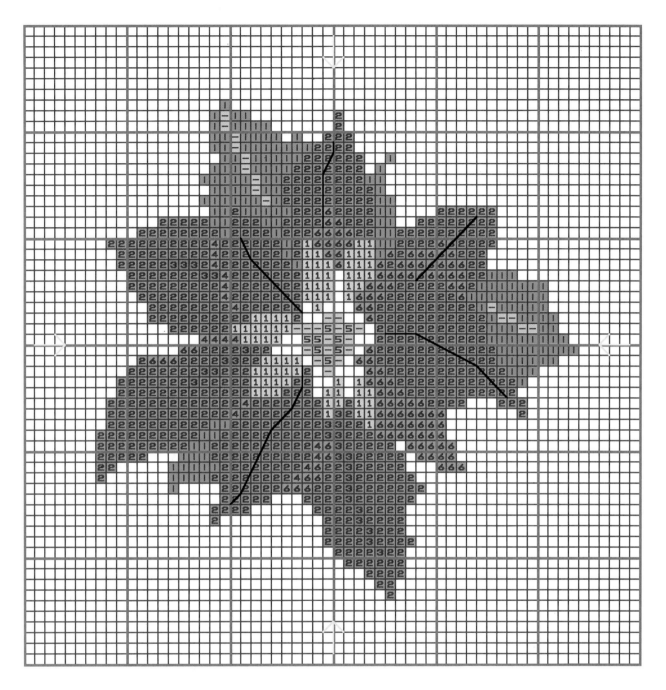

COLOR KEY

5	307	Buttercup Yellow	4	817	Scarlet
6	349	Bright Flame Red	–	966	Pale Laurel
1	352	Coral	I	988	Leaf Green
2	606	Flame Red	3	989	Medium Green

OUTLINING

━━━ Use one strand of 304 Deep Red for the veins in the flower petals.

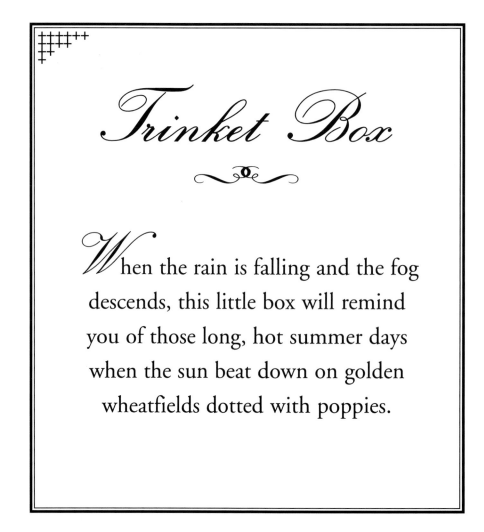

Trinket Box

When the rain is falling and the fog descends, this little box will remind you of those long, hot summer days when the sun beat down on golden wheatfields dotted with poppies.

YOU WILL NEED

to make one box, 3½ in (9 cm) in diameter

To stitch the design

8 x 8 in (20.3 x 20.3 cm) cream Aida cloth (14-count)
1 x 8.7 yd (8 m) skein of DMC 6-strand embroidery
    floss in each of the 8 colors listed in the Color Key
    and Outlining
Size 24 tapestry needle
Colored cotton thread for marking the guidelines

To assemble the lid of the bowl

6 x 6 in (15.2 x 15.2 cm) medium-weight iron-on white
    interfacing
Pencil
Scissors
3½ in (9 cm) diameter, purchased, frosted glass bowl.

STITCHING THE DESIGN

1. Baste guidelines with colored cotton thread to mark
   the center of the Aida before positioning it on your
   hoop or frame. This design will fit into a 6 in (15.2
   cm) embroidery hoop.
2. Join the arrows on the chart to find the center of the
   design and stitch the piece, using two strands of floss
   for all cross stitches. Outlining details are included.
3. Remove the guidelines and steam-press the worked
   piece flat after placing it facedown on a clean surface.
   If you are not using a steam iron, lay a damp cloth
   over the wrong side of the Aida before pressing it.

ASSEMBLING THE LID OF THE BOX

1. With the design facedown, iron the interfacing onto
   the wrong side of the Aida, making sure that you
   cover all the stitching. The interfacing adds stability
   to the fabric and prevents it from fraying when you
   trim the design to fit the lid.
2. Use the acetate provided as a template to ensure that
   the design is trimmed to the correct size. Center the
   acetate over your stitching so that the design shows to
   best advantage, then draw a pencil line around it.
3. Cut around the inside edge of the pencil line as
   carefully as you can so that the design fits without
   distortion.
4. Finish assembling the lid by following the supplier's
   instructions.

COLOR KEY					
1	310	Black	2	702	Emerald Green
3	564	Pale Laurel Green	4	725	Corn Yellow
⊟	606	Bright Red	5	989	Medium Green
Ⅱ	608	Orange Flame			

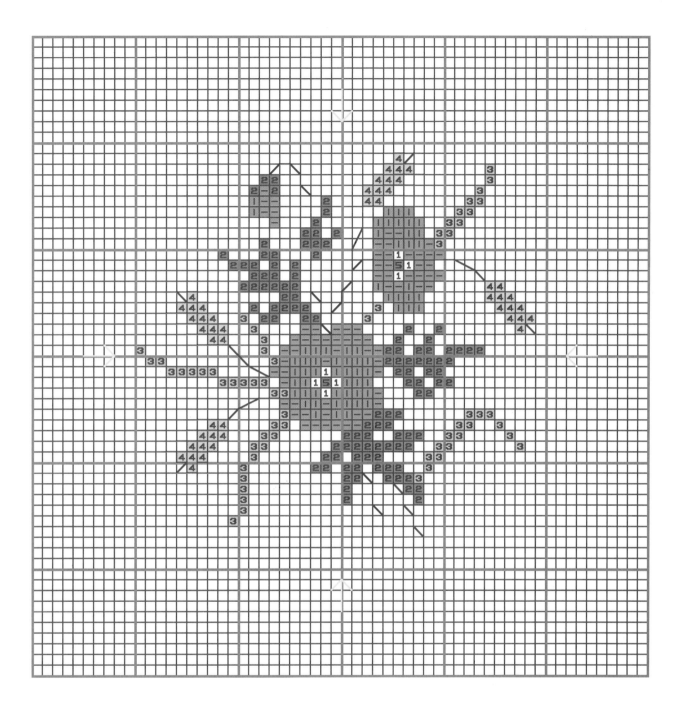

OUTLINING

▬	Use two strands of 702 Emerald Green for poppy stems.
▬	Use two strands of 564 Pale Laurel Green for the poppy stem.
▬	Use one strand of 782 Burnished Gold to outline the wheat and its stems.

Cosmetics Bag

This simple bag has been specially created to hold your essential makeup. Its cheerful design worked on bright red fabric will brighten up the dreariest of days!

YOU WILL NEED

to make one bag, finished size 6½ x 4½ in (16.5 x 11.5 cm) approx.

To stitch the design

12¾ x 7½ in (32.3 x 19 cm) red Aida cloth (14-count)
1 x 8.7 yd (8 m) skein of DMC 6-strand embroidery
    floss in each of the 3 colors listed in the Color Key
Size 24 tapestry needle
Colored cotton thread for marking the guidelines

To make the bag

12¾ x 7½ in (32.3 x 19 cm) red lining material
12¾ x 7½ in (32.3 x 19 cm) iron-on white quilted
    interfacing
1½ yd (137 cm) red bias binding, ⅝ in (1.4 cm) wide
Red cotton thread to match your binding
Sharp sewing needle
Pins
Scissors

STITCHING THE DESIGN

1. Mark the vertical guideline by folding the short side of the fabric in half and following the central thread.
2. To mark the horizontal guideline, count 30 squares from the bottom of the Aida and follow the thread between the 30th and 31st squares. The positioning of the design is especially critical in this project, and this method ensures correct placement.
3. You will see that the design is stitched toward the bottom of the fabric. The point where your guidelines cross remains the point where the center of the design should be positioned.
4. It is better to use a small tapestry frame for this design because the Aida is too large to fit comfortably into an embroidery hoop.
5. Join the arrows on the chart to find the center of the design and stitch the piece, using two strands of floss for all cross stitches.
6. Remove the guidelines and steam-press the worked piece flat after placing it facedown on a clean surface. If you are not using a steam iron, lay a damp cloth over the wrong side of the fabric before pressing it.

MAKING THE BAG

1. Iron the interfacing onto the lining material.
2. Turn the Aida facedown and place the other fabrics on top of it, with the lining material uppermost. Join the pieces of fabric together with pins, taking a ½ in (1.2 cm) seam from each edge. Hand- or machine-stitch along the seams and remove the pins.
3. Turn the design faceup and place pins at each side of the Aida on the thread marking the upper design edge.
4. With the design faceup and at the bottom, trim the seam allowance to ¼ in (6 mm) along the top edge only and attach bias binding (see Step 9, below) along top edge.
5. Place the Aida facedown and turn it so that the design now lies at the top.
6. To make the pocket of the bag, fold the bound edge up to the pins that mark the limit of your stitching. Baste stitches down each side of the pocket, following the existing seamlines, then hand- or machine-stitch once again along each seam. Remove the basting stitches and pins.
7. Trim all seam allowances to ¼ in (6 mm), and attach bias binding around the sides and top of the bag. At this point, you should fold over the cut ends of the binding by about ¼ in (6 mm) to prevent them fraying, and neaten them off by overcasting.
8. Fold the top of the bag over so that the design shows in front.
9. **To attach bias binding**
   a) Open out the folded edge at one edge of the binding and pin it in position on the right side of the fabric, matching the edge of the binding to the raw edges of the seam allowance(s). Secure the binding by hand- or machine-stitching along the seamline.
   b) Fold the binding over the raw edges onto the wrong side of the fabric, and hold it in position with pins or basting stitches before neatly hemming it to finish.

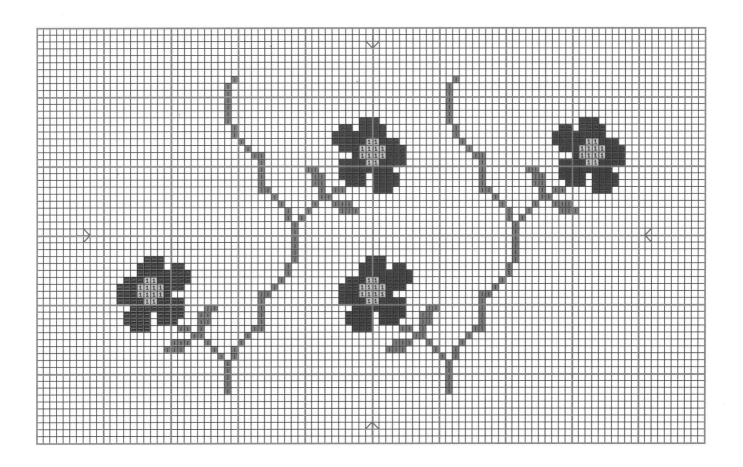

COLOR KEY					
▬	792	Deep Blue	1	992	Jade Green
1	972	Bright Yellow			

Victorian Handkerchief Sachet

Antique linen is trimmed with lace to re-create a simple but treasured possession from times past – a keepsake once found on every lady's dressing table.

YOU WILL NEED

to make one sachet, finished size 7½ x 7½ in (19 x 19 cm) approx.

To stitch the design

14 x 14 in (35.5 x 35.5 cm) antique evenweave linen (28 threads to the inch)

1 x 8.7 yd (8 m) skein of DMC 6-strand embroidery floss in each of the 5 colors listed in the Color Key and Outlining

Size 26 tapestry needle

2 lengths of different-colored cotton thread for marking guidelines

To make the sachet

11¾ x 11¾ in (29.8 x 29.8 cm) plain white cotton lining

48 in (122 cm) white lace trimming, ¾ in (2 cm) wide approx.

DMC Blanc 6-strand embroidery floss

Button, ⅜ in (9 mm) wide approx.

White cotton thread

Sharp sewing needle

Pins

Scissors

STITCHING THE DESIGN

1. Mark guidelines on your linen showing the perimeter of your working area. To do this, measure in 1⅝ in (4.1 cm) from each edge of the linen, and tack guidelines in colored cotton thread [Color A] along the nearest threads. You will have a square of 10¾ x 10¾ in (27.3 x 27.3 cm) in the center of the fabric.

2. To mark guidelines showing the centers of the designs, measure in 3¼ in (8.2 cm) from each edge of the linen, and baste guidelines in a different colored cotton thread [Color B] along the nearest threads. You will now also have an inner square of 7½ x 7½ in (19 x 19 cm). The points where the guidelines in Color B cross are the points where your stitching should be centered.

3. Join the arrows on the chart to find the center of the design and then stitch it in each corner of the linen using two strands of floss for all cross stitches. Outlining details are included.

4. To make sure that you stitch the design correctly in each corner, you may find it easier to turn the fabric around so that you can work each corner in the same way.

5. Remove the guidelines in Color B only and steam-press the worked piece flat after placing it facedown on a clean surface.

MAKING THE SACHET

1. Trim the linen to 11¾ x 11¾ in (29.8 x 29.8 cm), making sure that the working area remains centrally positioned.

2. Following the guidelines all the way around, fold over ½ in (1.2 cm) of linen onto the wrong side and baste it close to the edge. Remove the colored guidelines and trim the turned edge close to the basting.

3. Take the cotton lining and fold over ½ in (1.2 cm) around all sides. Baste the folded side close to the edge, and trim it close to your stitching.

4. Place the linen and its lining wrong sides together, and pin them all around. Stitch along the edges with white cotton thread so that the two pieces of fabric are securely joined and remove all pins and basting.

5. Attach lace trim (see Step 8, below) along all four sides.

6. Turn the linen facedown, and bring the four corners to the center to form the sachet.

7. Keeping the corners in position with small weights, sew the button onto one of the corners, and, using all six strands of the blanc 6-strand embroidery floss, fix loops on each of the other three corners, just large enough for the button to pass through.

8. To attach lace trim

a) Pin the trim to the right side of your fabric so that half of its width will show. Cut off any excess length, and hem the lace into position, removing the pins as you go. You will need to make small miters at each corner so that they lie as neatly as possible.

b) Turn the fabric over and fold the second half of the trim onto the wrong side, fixing it into position in the same way.

COLOR KEY					
⊡	553	Violet	⊡	701	Bright Green
⊟	603	Deep Pink	⊡	744	Rich Yellow

OUTLINING

— Use one strand of 699 Dark Bright Green for the stems.

This same design is stitched in each of the four corners of the sachet.

Rambling Rose Glasses Case

*E*asy to stitch and very practical,
this decorative canvas case will provide
genuine protection for your
reading glasses or sunglasses.

YOU WILL NEED

to make one case, finished size 6 x 3 in (15.2 x 7.6 cm) approx.

To stitch the design

2 pieces of white single thread interlock canvas (18 holes
  to the inch) cut to 9 x 6 in (22.9 x 15.2 cm)
1 x 8.7 yd (8 m) skein of DMC 6-strand embroidery
  floss in each of the colors listed in the Color Key,
  except shade 327 Mauve
6 x 8.7 yd (8 m) skeins of DMC 6-strand embroidery
  floss, shade 327 Mauve
Size 24 tapestry needle
Colored cotton thread for marking the guidelines

To make the case

2 pieces of white felt cut to 9 x 6 in (22.9 x 15.2 cm)
Double-faced tape, ½ in (1.2 cm) wide
Scissors

STITCHING THE DESIGN

1. Take one piece of canvas and baste guidelines with colored cotton thread to mark the center. You should find that the canvas is stiff enough to work only in your hand, but you may wish to fix it to a small tapestry frame. Do not use an embroidery hoop!
2. Join the arrows on the chart to find the center of the design and stitch the piece, using three strands of floss for all cross stitches.
3. Stitch each cross stitch over one intersection of canvas only (see Basics of Cross Stitch, page 14).
4. Work the design in the same way on the second piece of canvas. Label front and back.
5. Remove the guidelines from both pieces of canvas, and gently ease them flat and square by pulling at each corner. You should not use steam on canvas unless it has been professionally blocked.

TO MAKE THE CASE

1. Begin with the front of the case. Measure ½ in (1.2 cm) away from the stitching on all four sides and trim the canvas to size.
2. Turn the design facedown and place a strip of double-faced tape along the ½ in (1.2 cm) edges for turning at both sides of the canvas. Fold the edges for turning down behind the stitching, making sure that the tape holds securely. Tape down the folded edges at the top and bottom in the same way.
3. Place one piece of white felt over the canvas and trim it to size – it is important for the finished look of the case that the felt does not overlap the canvas at any point. Put the felt aside.
4. With the design still facedown, place double-faced tape very close to all the edges of the canvas. Position the felt, pressing it onto the tape.
5. Overcast the raw edge at the top of the design using three strands of 327 Mauve, and taking care to catch the edge of the felt into your stitches. Do not overcast the other edges at this point.
6. Repeat Steps 1–5 with the back of the case.
7. Place the two canvas pieces with the designs right side out, and overcast the front and back of the case together around the sides and bottom, using three strands of 327 Mauve.

COLOR KEY					
1	319	Dark Green	5	966	Pale Laurel
7	327	Mauve	6	973	Bright Yellow
3	604	Rose Pink	I	988	Leaf Green
4	605	Pale Rose	=	989	Medium Green
2	921	Terra-cotta			

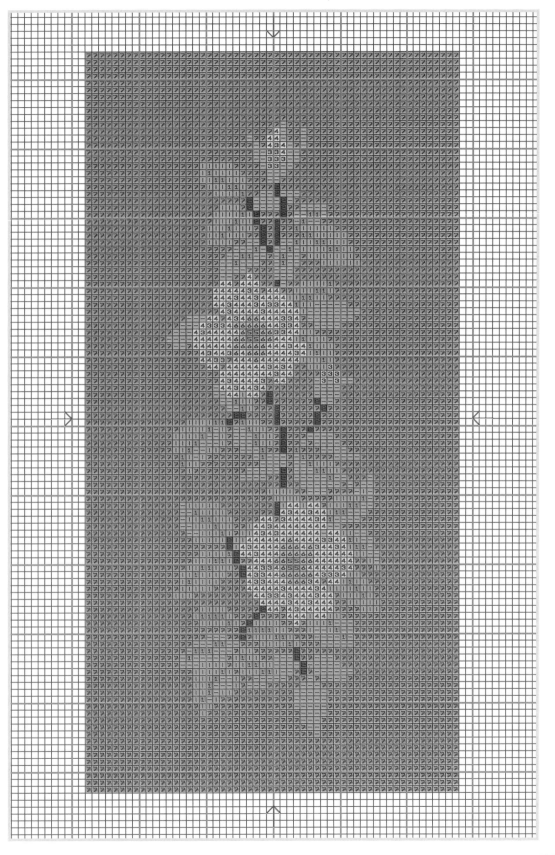

Herbal Pillow

After making this beautiful pillow, fill it with aromatic herbs and place it on your bed. It will help you to relax and sleep soundly every night.

YOU WILL NEED

to make one pillow, finished size 10 x 8 in (25.4 x 20.3 cm) approx.

To stitch the design

12 x 10 in (30.5 x 25.4 cm) white evenweave cotton (26 threads to the inch)

1 x 8.7 yd (8 m) skein of DMC 6-strand embroidery floss in each of the 18 colors listed in the Color Key and Outlining

Size 24 tapestry needle

Colored cotton thread for marking the guidelines

To make the pillow

11 x 9 in (28 x 22.9 cm) plain white cotton fabric (e.g., fine sheeting)

48 in (122 cm) double-sided white satin ribbon, ⅛ in (3mm) wide

Large-eyed tapestry needle or weaving needle

White cotton thread

Sharp sewing needle

Pins

Scissors

For the cushion pad

2 pieces plain white cotton lawn fabric, both 11 x 9 in (28 x 22.9 cm)

Batting

Your chosen fragrant herb mixture

STITCHING THE DESIGN

1. Baste guidelines with colored cotton thread to mark the center of the evenweave before positioning it on a small frame. This design is too large to fit comfortably in an embroidery hoop.

2. Join the arrows on the chart to find the center of the design and stitch the piece, using two strands of floss for all cross stitches. Outlining details are included.

3. Remove the guidelines and steam-press the worked piece flat after placing it facedown on a clean surface. If you are not using a steam iron, lay a damp cloth over the wrong side of the cotton before pressing it.

MAKING THE PILLOW

1. Turn the design faceup and trim the evenweave to 11 x 9 in (28 x 22.9 cm), making sure that the design remains centrally positioned.

2. Measure in 2 in (5 cm) from each edge and carefully remove the two nearest threads from the evenweave. This creates the space for the ribbon to go through.

3. Cut 2 x 15 in (38 cm) lengths and 2 x 13 in (33 cm) lengths from the ribbon, and thread a 13 in (33 cm) length through the large-eyed tapestry needle or weaving needle.

4. Place the needle in the space created by the removed threads 2 in (5 cm) from the left-hand side of the evenweave, and weave the ribbon across the fabric. Work under five threads to start and then over eight threads on the right side of the fabric, repeating this all the way across. Be very careful not to distort the shape of the fabric by pulling the ribbon too firmly.

5. Weave ribbon across the remaining three sides in the same way.

6. Pin your backing fabric on top of the evenweave so that the right sides are together. Baste a seamline ½ in (1.2 cm) from each edge, making sure that you secure the ribbons in place. Leave an opening of about 6 in (15.2 cm) along one side so that you can insert the cushion pad. Hand- or machine-stitch along the seam and remove the basting stitches.

7. Trim the seam allowance to ¼ in (6 mm). You may wish to overcast the raw edges of the allowance to prevent them from fraying.

8. Turn the pillow right side out, keeping the seams as flat as possible, and insert the cushion pad (see Step 9, below). Slipstitch the opening closed along seamline.

9. **To make a cushion pad**

a) Place the two pieces of cotton lawn together and stitch a seam ½ in (1.2 cm) from each side, leaving a 5 in (12.7 cm) opening along one side to insert the batting. Trim the seam allowance to ¼ in (6 mm) and turn the fabric right side out.

b) Fill the pad with batting and the fragrant herb mixture to your required thickness, then slipstitch the opening closed.

COLOR KEY

◇		Blanc	1	742	Orange
∐	211	Pale Lilac	⊠	832	Dark Mustard
6	367	Forest Green	⦂⦂	841	Dark Beige
5	368	Medium Forest Green	7	842	Beige
4	472	Pale Spring Green	=	963	Pale Pink
−	554	Violet	3	3345	Dark Green
9	725	Yellow	2	3347	Medium Green
8	727	Pale Yellow	⦙⦙	3348	Moss Green

OUTLINING

—— Use two strands of 3348 Moss Green for the violet stems .
—— Use one strand of 648 Stone Gray around the peony flowers.
—— Use one strand of 834 Golden Maize around the marigold flowers.

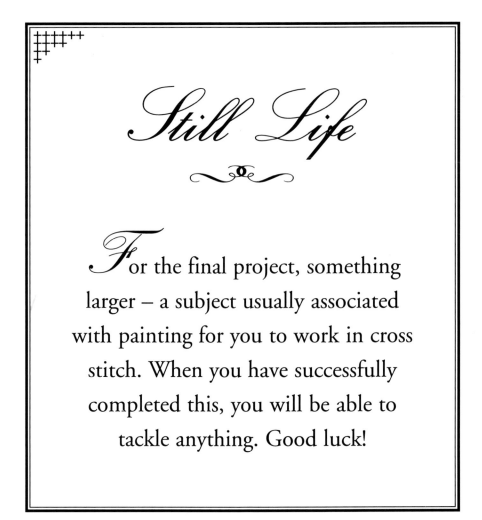

Still Life

For the final project, something larger – a subject usually associated with painting for you to work in cross stitch. When you have successfully completed this, you will be able to tackle anything. Good luck!

YOU WILL NEED

to make one design size 5½ x 4¼ in (14 x 10.7 cm) approx.

To stitch the design

12 x 10 in (30.5 x 25.4 cm) cream Aida cloth (14-count)
1 x 8.7 yd (8 m) skein of DMC 6-strand embroidery floss in each of the 29 colors listed in the Color Key
Size 24 tapestry needle
Colored cotton thread for marking the guidelines

To mount the embroidery

7½ x 6½ in (19 x 16.5 cm) white mounting board
Pins
Double-faced tape, 1 in (2.5 cm) wide
Masking tape, 1 in (2.5 cm) wide

STITCHING THE DESIGN

1. Baste guidelines with colored cotton thread to mark the center of the Aida before positioning it on your frame. This design does not fit comfortably into an embroidery hoop.
2. Join the arrows on the chart to find the center of the design and stitch the piece, using two strands of floss for all cross stitches. Outlining details are included.
3. Do not remove the guidelines, but steam-press the worked piece flat after placing it facedown on a clean surface. If you are not using a steam iron, lay a damp cloth over the wrong side of the Aida before pressing.

MOUNTING THE EMBROIDERY

1. Trim the Aida to 9½ x 8½ in (24 x 21.5 cm) making sure that the design remains centrally positioned.
2. With the design facedown, center the mounting board over the Aida. To do this, mark the mid point on all four sides of the board, and align these points with the guidelines on your fabric.
3. Place a pin into the thickness of the board at each of these four points, joining the Aida and the board together. Turn the board over so that you can see the embroidery.
4. Starting at the top of the design, insert pins at regular intervals into the thickness of the board to stretch the Aida. Work from the midpoint out to each side, and keep the fabric as flat and square as you can. This is done by keeping the thread of the Aida nearest the edge as straight as possible and pulling the fabric so that it lies flat but does not distort.
5. Repeat the process around the other three sides of the design (*working top-side-bottom-side*), but on these sides work from a pinned corner to the opposite corner. You may find that your central pins will need to be moved as the embroidery is stretched.
6. When you have pinned all four sides, make any necessary adjustments, remove the guidelines, and place the design facedown.
7. Cut a strip of double-faced tape 7½ in (19 cm) long, and lay it on the board along one of the sides. Fold the Aida over so that it is held securely by the tape, then repeat the process around the other three sides (*working side-side-top-bottom*), with the tape at the top and bottom being 6½ in (16.5 cm) long. The corners will have an extra thickness, but keep them flat.
8. Cover the raw edges of the fabric with strips of masking tape and remove all pins.

This method of mounting embroidery is suitable for small designs, such as those in this book. If you wish to mount large designs, or embroidery worked on heavy-weight fabrics, we recommend that the work be done by a professional stretcher and framer, who will probably use lacing thread.

OUTLINING

- Use one strand of 828 Sky Blue around the yellow pansy.
- Use two strands of 310 Black in the center of the red pansy.
- Use two strands of 580 Dark Moss Green for the flower stems.

COLOR KEY								
⊟		Blanc	◣	554	Pale Violet	④	892	Deep Pink
⌂	210	Lilac	◿	580	Dark Moss Green	⑤	894	Medium Pink
▽	211	Pale Lilac	①	726	Yellow	Λ	900	Burnt Orange
◢	309	Carmine Rose	‖	740	Bright Orange	⊠	947	Orange Flame
③	310	Black	⊟	762	Light Gray	◈	977	Tangerine
②	413	Dark Gray	⦂	775	Pale Sea Blue	⑨	3078	Pale Buttercup Yellow
‖	415	Gray	⊞	781	Dark Gold	◥	3325	Sea Blue
⑧	471	Moss Green	◗◗	783	Gold	◩	3347	Grass Green
⊠	552	Dark Violet	⓪	826	Kingfisher Blue	◰	3348	Pale Grass Green
⁄	553	Violet	⊡	828	Sky Blue			

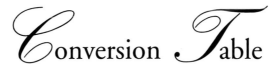

Conversion Table

The table below lists the nearest equivalent colors in two other major ranges of Stranded Floss.

It is impossible to give exact alternatives between different ranges, so the conversions are not perfect matches but are in our opinion the closest substitutes available.

The table is intended as a guide only. If possible, compare actual skeins before making a decision.

DMC	Anchor	Madeira	DMC	Anchor	Madeira
Blanc	1	White	369	213	1701
209	109	0804	400	351	2305
210	108	0802	402	313	2307
211	342	0801	413	401	1713
301	349	2306	415	398	1802
304	47	0511	420	375	2105
307	289	0104	422	373	2102
309	42	0507	433	371	2008
310	403	Black	434	310	2009
316	969	0808	435	365	2010
317	235	1714	436	363	2011
318	399	1802	437	368	1910
319	246	1313	445	288	0103
327	101	0714	470	266	1502
333	119	0903	471	280	1501
341	117	0901	472	253	1414
349	13	0212	519	168	1105
351	10	0214	535	401	1809
352	9	0303	552	101	0713
367	262	1312	553	98	0712
368	261	1310	554	96	0711

DMC	Anchor	Madeira	DMC	Anchor	Madeira
562	210	1312	712	387	2101
563	204	1207	718	88	0707
564	203	1208	725	306	0113
580	268	1504	726	295	0109
597	168	1110	727	293	0110
598	928	1111	738	942	2013
603	62	0701	740	316	0203
604	55	0614	741	304	0201
605	50	0613	742	303	0114
606	335	0209	743	297	0113
608	333	0206	744	301	0112
610	905	2003	746	275	0101
611	898	2107	747	158	1104
612	832	2108	762	397	1804
613	831	2109	772	264	1604
642	392	1905	775	975	1001
644	830	1907	776	24	0503
645	400	1801	778	968	0808
648	900	1813	781	308	2213
676	891	2208	782	307	2212
680	901	2210	783	306	2211
699	923	1303	792	177	0905
700	228	1304	798	131	0911
701	244	1305	800	128	0907
702	227	1306	813	160	1003
703	226	1307	817	47	0211
704	256	1308	822	390	1908

DMC	Anchor	Madeira	DMC	Anchor	Madeira
826	161	1012	989	256	1401
828	158	1101	991	189	1204
832	907	2202	992	187	1202
834	874	2204	993	186	1201
841	378	1911	996	433	1103
842	376	1910	3012	854	1606
890	218	1314	3021	382	1904
891	35	0411	3022	393	1903
892	28	0412	3024	391	1901
894	26	0504	3031	905	2003
900	326	0208	3033	388	1909
921	338	0311	3047	852	2205
922	1001	0310	3064	883	2312
943	188	1203	3078	292	0102
945	881	2313	3325	159	1002
947	330	0205	3341	328	0307
956	40	0413	3345	268	1406
957	52	0612	3347	267	1408
962	54	0609	3348	265	1409
963	23	0608	3350	69	0603
966	206	1209	3608	86	0709
972	303	0107	3609	85	0710
973	290	0106	3705	35	0410
976	309	2302	3706	33	0409
977	313	2301	3708	26	0408
987	244	1403			
988	257	1402			

The basic items used in making up some of the projects in this book were kindly supplied by the following company, who will be pleased to forward goods by mail-order:

Framecraft Miniatures Ltd
372-376 Summer Lane
Hockley
Birmingham
B19 3QA
Great Britain
Telephone: 0121 212-0551

ADDRESSES OF *FRAMECRAFT* DISTRIBUTORS IN NORTH AMERICA:

Anne Brinkley Designs, Inc.
761 Palmer Avenue
Holmdel, N.J. 97733
U.S.A.
Telephone: 908 530-5432

Gay Bowles Sales, Inc.
P.O. Box 1060
Janesville, Wis. 53547
U.S.A.
Telephone: 608 754-9212

Danish Art Needlework
P.O. Box 442
Lethbridge
Alberta T1J 3Z1
Canada
Telephone: 403 327-9855

Coats & Clark
P.O. Box 27067
Dept CO1
Greenville, S.C. 29616
U.S.A.
Telephone: 803 234-0103

Madeira Marketing Ltd
600 East 9th Street
Michigan City, Ind. 46360
U.S.A.
Telephone: 219 873-1000

*S*uppliers